Allison Bottke has once again written a bo[ok] Much like her acclaimed *Setting Boundarie.* long-awaited follow-up will captivate you Allison's transparency is powerful. Relating book almost took my breath away. As a mother with troubled adult children, I often feel no matter the age of my children, the labor pains never seem to end. *How to Connect with Your Troubled Adult Children* is insightful, informative and inspiring—a true page-turner. At last someone is addressing the opioid epidemic and the associated issues of emotional and mental illness boldly and without fear.

~**Sharon Hill,** founder, On Call Prayer Ministries and senior executive vice president of Christian Women in Media Association

The pain of a parent can run very deep, believe me. I know this personally. Many of us are facing serious relationship challenges that must be addressed. Allison writes candidly and openly from her own experiences and broken heart. Her brutal honesty combined with practical insight has produced a self-help book that is concise and will prove effective for so many. *How to Connect with Your Troubled Adult Children* is a must-read for hurting parents.

~**Dr. Victoria Sarvadi,** teacher of Hebraic studies and Selah finalist author of *Just a Little Girl*

Allison Bottke has learned how to live a healthy life—a sane life—despite the drama a troubled adult child often brings into their relationship. Her courageous candidness and words of wisdom give parents the strength and hope needed to make choices that will benefit everyone involved. Help awaits in the pages of what is certain to be a landmark book. *How to Connect with Your Troubled Adult Children* will empower millions of weary, broken-hearted parents and be a catalyst for the restoration of families all over the world.

~**Andy Lee,** author of *A Mary Like Me*

No one understands the pain...the effort...the hoped-for joy of connecting with troubled adult children as much as those who have walked the path. Those who have fought the fight. Those whose knees are calloused from hours in prayer. Those who have put their trust in the Supreme Parent, but who also know that, as in all battles, we soldiers have armor to don. We have ammunition to use. Allison Bottke knows. She understands. Trust me; you can trust her with this.

~**Eva Marie Everson,** bestselling, award-winning author, www.evamarieeversonauthor.com

What do I do? Who do I call? Why is this happening? Parents of troubled adult children are often left feeling bamboozled. While we often support the decision to give our kids "tough love," we seldom shine the same critical light on ourselves. In her newest book, Allison gives us—the adult parents—"tough love." She lays it out as you've never heard it before! Practical, hopeful, and sometimes hard to hear, her SANITY strategies must be implemented to keep parents healthy, financially secure, and most important, spiritually and mentally sane!

~**Dr. Euphemia Gans,** author of "What Is a Learning Organization?"
Ethics and Critical Thinking Journal

In *How to Connect with Your Troubled Adult Children*, Allison Bottke captures the painful reality that many of the children we once knew are no longer with us. As she writes, "Layer by layer, we see our kids buried along with our hopes and dreams for them." Addressing the painful topics of drug abuse and emotional and mental illness, this is a book whose time has come. With her trademark tenacity and transparency, Allison's advice stoked the fire of hope and joy in my spirit. Once again, Allison has given us a fresh perspective on the reappearance of Jesus and the possibility of restoration even in the most difficult passages of life when we love a troubled adult child. She's been there and knows of what she speaks.

~**Jonathan Settel,** international messianic recording artist

What can you do when parenting gets painfully complicated? When substance abuse has transformed the child you love into a stranger you don't recognize? How can your actions be helpful and not harmful when your adult child's mental, emotional, physical, and spiritual health issues are driving you to despair? When your child has reached (or long since passed) the point of independence, it's difficult to know what your "help" as a parent should look like. What is God really calling you to do? In a world desperate for answers and direction, there is no greater champion than Allison Bottke for broken-hearted parents who struggle in challenging relationships with their adult children. Allison bares her soul in an inspiring book that is destined to change lives and restore relationships. *How to Connect with Your Troubled Adult Children* will become the go-to resource for Christian parents, grandparents, counselors, and therapists as it addresses drug addiction and emotional and mental illness from a spiritual perspective.

~**Ann White,** founder, executive director of Courage for Life and author of
Courage for Life and *She Is Strong and Courageous*

How to Connect with Your ^Adult Children

Troubled

ALLISON BOTTKE

HARVEST HOUSE PUBLISHERS
EUGENE, OREGON

Cover by Aesthetic Soup, Shakoppe, Minnesota

Cover photos © www_logo_expert / Shutterstock

SETTING BOUNDARIES is a registered trademark of The Hawkins Children's LLC. Harvest House Publishers, Inc. is the exclusive licensee of the federally registered trademark SETTING BOUNDARIES.

Published in association with the literary agency of The Steve Laube Agency, LLC, 24 W. Camelback Rd. A-635, Phoenix, Arizona 85013.

The names and identifying information of the people discussed in this book have been changed to protect their identities and to respect their confidentiality.

This book is not intended to take the place of professional medical or psychological advice. Neither the author nor the publisher assumes any liability for possible adverse consequences as a result of the information contained herein.

How to Connect with Your Troubled Adult Children
Copyright © 2018 by Allison Bottke
Published by Harvest House Publishers
Eugene, Oregon 97408
www.harvesthousepublishers.com

ISBN 978-0-7369-6239-1 (pbk.)
ISBN 978-0-7369-6240-7 (eBook)

Library of Congress Cataloging-in-Publication Data

Names: Bottke, Allison author.
Title: How to connect with your troubled adult children / Allison Bottke.
Description: Eugene, Oregon : Harvest House Publishers, [2018] | Includes
    bibliographical references.
Identifiers: LCCN 2018030161 (print) | LCCN 2018037850 (ebook) | ISBN
    9780736962407 (ebook) | ISBN 9780736962391 | ISBN
    9780736962391¬q(paperback) | ISBN 9780736962407¬q(eBook)
Subjects: LCSH: Parent and adult child--Religious aspects--Christianity.
Classification: LCC BV4529 (ebook) | LCC BV4529 .B6748 2018 (print) | DDC
    248.8/45--dc23
LC record available at https://lccn.loc.gov/2018030161

Printed in the United States of America

18 19 20 21 22 23 24 25 26 / BP-SK / 10 9 8 7 6 5 4 3 2 1

Mom
Who taught me compassion and character by example.

Christopher
No matter what, I will always love you, my precious son.

Lori Jo Eleazer
A living, breathing blessing from God.

Parents and Grandparents
The reason I write about broken hearts and lost dreams.
You will always be the wind beneath my wings.
Your faith, hope, and trust in God is what empowers and
strengthens me.

Never forget…
"With God all things are possible."
Matthew 19:26

Contents

Chapter 1

This Isn't How Life Is Supposed to Be

Ilt may sound silly, but I can't tell you how many times over the years I've stood in front of a card rack trying—and failing—to find an appropriate card for my son.

You see, we live in a world where mass marketing rules the consumer landscape, so we are showered with Hallmark-moment images and words that determine how, when, and why we should convey our affection for people we love. There is, however, no card on the rack for those of us who have seriously troubled adult children whose dangerous choices and traumatic, sometimes toxic lives have turned our own upside down.

For these kids, there isn't a greeting card that works. Ever. The effusive words of pride, appreciation, and love just don't fit. On any occasion. Happy Birthday...to a son who has so many felony charges on his record that he will never be able to find a job, get a driver's license, or even vote—and blames everyone but himself? Merry Christmas... to a daughter whose drug addiction has cost her not only her marriage but the custody of her children as well? What card speaks of how you feel about a child whose legal troubles have cost you all your savings and most likely your retirement too?

It's been years since I've been able to buy a preprinted card for my son. So I've resorted to sending humorous cards, or I buy the ones with blank interiors and write something as appropriate as possible, all the while aching inside because what I really long to do is buy the sweet, sappy, sentimental cards that a mom should be able to buy for her child. You know, the ones that say, *I'm so incredibly proud of you* and *You're the child every parent dreams of.*

I can't say those things—and sometimes I hate myself for feeling that way.

This isn't how life is supposed to be.

How Did We Get Here?

It doesn't matter how long ago it was, a mother always remembers the day every one of her children is born. The same can be said for many fathers. Childbirth truly is an experience unlike any other, making the relationship between parent and child one of indescribable connection and profound possibility.

As a teenage mom, though, I had struggles with my own issues and demons, but when the delivery room nurse placed that tiny bundle in my arms, I was immediately connected to my son in a way I had never imagined possible. As the days, months, and years passed, what I wanted most was for my sweet boy to know how much I loved him and that I would always be there for him. I worked hard, played hard, and, through it all, provided everything I thought my son wanted or needed—including rescuing him whenever trouble called. After all, wasn't that my job as his mom?

Sadly, my own personal issues—including painful memories from a traumatic past—often drove me to make unhealthy parenting choices. Time after time, thinking I was helping, I bailed my son out of difficult situations, derailing many life lessons he might have learned from the natural consequences of his actions.

God has plans for all of us, and some of those plans involve pain. Pain we need to experience to learn the spiritual growth lessons God wants to teach us.

It took years before I understood that I was playing God every time I swooped in to rescue my son and, in essence, accept responsibility for his choices. I wasn't helping Chris at all. I was merely enabling him to continue his increasingly inappropriate behavior without having to deal with any consequences. I didn't quickly make the connection that painful life experiences help to shape our character. And I certainly didn't realize that all my unhealthy rescuing was being fueled and motivated by a spiritual emptiness in my own heart.

By the time I realized how I had contributed to our dysfunctional parent/child relationship, my only child was in his thirties, already in and out of jail numerous times, and deeply in bondage to an IV heroin addiction.

I know many of you have similar stories—some less challenging, others far worse—and my heart breaks for each of you.

We are all doing the best we can. But I think with a shift in our perspective, our best can become better.

Hard Life Lessons

My personal faith journey started late in life: I was 35. Since then, I've tried to do my best to view life and the lessons it teaches through a lens of faith in God. Yet there is one lesson I've been hard-pressed to learn despite the many opportunities God has given me.

This lesson I very much wanted to learn—and still want to master—is how to connect with my troubled adult son in a healthy way that is more helpful than hurtful, more empowering than enabling. In a way that will help him to see that he needs to make better choices—before it's too late.

The thing is, I did everything I knew how to do, and I know you did too. We have all tried to be really good parents, but the way our children have changed and the things they've done have left us shocked, embarrassed, angry, guilty, hopeless, and feeling so alone.

We cry out to God, but sometimes it's hard to hear His voice.

A Painful Reality

So let me share a lesson I *have* learned: It's impossible to move forward if we're tethered to something that's holding us back.

Many of us, for instance, are hanging on to what could have been.

We had so many dreams for our young children; we saw their incredible potential.

But as they grew up, something went wrong. In many cases, horribly wrong.

What happened to our kids?

Pain happened, and it came in many ways, from many sources, in a variety of settings. Then sin happened as our children desperately attempted to relieve the pain. And, finally, drugs happened. Alcohol happened. Emotional instability and mental illness happened. Incarceration happened. Traumatic situations and circumstances happened. Drama, chaos, and crisis happened. And sometimes, character void of conscience happened.

Layer by layer, our kids were being buried—along with our hopes and dreams for them.

The painful reality is that the children we once knew are gone. Much like a tornado that touches down, roars forward, and tears up everything in its path, many of our troubled adult children have left a wide path of damage and destruction in their wake. We've been reacting to their poor choices for so long that we've run out of patience, compassion, money, and faith that they will ever change. We will always love them, but as things stand now, we don't like them very much.

If we want to learn how to connect with our troubled adult children, we must let go of our old dreams for them and our unreasonable expectations. We can't go back and re-parent all over again, hoping for a different outcome. Instead, we must find a way to push through the pain and go forward. It's time to change our perspective on our lives and adjust our expectations as we formulate an honest appraisal of both who our adult children are today and of their ability to live independently in the future.

Most important, we need to understand what role God is calling us to have in their troubled lives.

White Flags

One distressed parent of a bipolar daughter—who refused to take medication and disrupted the lives of everyone she came in contact with—said to me, "Allison, I'm ready to wave a white flag of surrender.

I can't take this anymore. It's killing me. This isn't how life is supposed to be!"

She's right. God didn't intend for us to live this way. That's why it's time for us to take a new approach, to change the lens through which we view the connection we have—or don't have—with our troubled adult child. There does come a time when we need to surrender—to stop, step back, and reassess the entire situation. A time when seeking professional advice and wise counsel may be needed. A time to chart a new course and develop a different plan of action. And a time to prayerfully consider what God wants our parenting role to look like now and in the future.

Parents, the time is now! It is time for us to willingly surrender and release our children—even if we feel as if we've done this again and again through the years—so that God can do in their hearts and lives what He does best: rescue and redeem. And please hear me when I say this: To surrender does not mean you've given up. When you reach this point and realize what you're doing isn't working, the important truth to remember is that God will never stop working.

Perhaps He's just been waiting for you—and me—to get out of the way.

A Mother's Fear

With dinner finished and the dishes done, Brenda was tired. She desperately wanted to get off her feet after what had been a long day. She worked part-time through a local temp agency, and while most of the assignments she took were secretarial, last week and this one were different. She was up at 4:00 a.m. to make a 5:00 a.m.-to-noon shift at a potato chip factory in Minneapolis.

"It's a two-week assignment," her supervisor said. "Are you interested?"

"Absolutely!" Brenda said without hesitation. The pay was unusually good, and she needed the extra money to help her daughter. However, standing on her feet every day for eight hours in front of a conveyor belt was harder than Brenda anticipated.

Lord, I'm feeling every one of my 55 years this week. Please help me get through this.

Brenda felt a tightness in her lower back as she bent over to pick up the toys scattered around the living room. "Girls, please help Grandma clean up before your mommy gets here!"

At five and six, her granddaughters were definitely old enough to pick up after themselves, but Brenda was finding it increasingly difficult to enforce rules at her home that the girls weren't required to follow in their own. Her daughter, Carla, had a hard time taking care of herself, let alone two active youngsters, and the only structure the girls had was here at Grandma's house.

Life had always been hard for Carla. Painfully shy and insecure as a child, she had also struggled with depression. Even early on Brenda felt certain Carla had other emotional and mental health issues as well. When Carla started acting out as a teenager, Brenda first suspected drugs were the reason, but now she wasn't sure. Although she didn't have proof, Brenda suspected the volatile mood swings and periods of deep sadness were quite possibly bipolar episodes. For years, Brenda begged Carla to see a doctor and get help, even offering to pay for both the visit and any medication that was prescribed.

"Don't be silly! I'm fine," Carla used to laugh. Now, any mention of her suspicions to Carla caused such rage and anger that Brenda was afraid to say anything. So she did what she could to keep things on an even keel, fervently praying that God would open her daughter's eyes to the bad decisions she was making and the ominous trajectory of her life.

In addition to her role as prayer warrior, Brenda was her daughter's go-to babysitter. The girls had been coming to Grandma's house for years, and their visits ranged from overnight stays to weekends. The last time Carla was in rehab, though, the two girls spent the entire summer with Brenda. Then there was the time that Brenda hated to think about: Carla was in jail for six months, and the girls shuffled between Brenda's house and the homes of relatives on their father's side.

A side note: Five-year-old Tiffany and six-year-old Brittany had different fathers. One was sporadically in the picture, and the other was serving a 15-year sentence in a federal correctional facility in Arizona. Carla was never married to either man.

Things, however, were looking up for Carla and the girls since she completed beauty school and recently got a job at a high-end salon in the nearby Mall of America. Brenda was excited and hopeful that this new job might be just what Carla needed to turn her life around.

"Grandma, Tiffany pulled my hair!" Brittany shouted.

"Liar! I did not. *You* pulled *my* hair!" Tiffany shouted back.

"Girls, please! Stop it right now and get your backpacks ready. Your mom will be here any minute!" *Dear Jesus, You know I love these babies, but I just don't have the energy or patience I used to have…* Brenda silently prayed.

She had agreed to pick the girls up from school that day and keep them until 7:00 p.m. because the salon was sending Carla to a training program.

"Where's Mommy?" Tiffany whined. *Good question*, Brenda thought. Her exhaustion was now being overshadowed by a growing headache… when her phone rang.

"Hi, Mom. Sorry I'm late. Tell the girls I'll be there in a half hour. I got tied up."

A half hour? It was already after eight, and the girls had school in the morning. Brenda herself had to be up in a few hours.

"Carla, you said you'd be here at 7:00…"

"I know that, Mother, but I said, I got tied up! I'll be there as soon as I can, and I've got good news! Bye!"

Good news… Brenda hoped it was something work related, but the high-pitched tone and rapid-fire staccato of her daughter's words sent red flags flying.

When Carla finally walked in at 9:30 with a young man whom Brenda had never met, the evening quickly went even farther downhill. Carla was high or drunk or maybe both. Brenda couldn't tell, but she was afraid for her daughter and hated for the girls to see their mother like this.

"Mom, this is Ben. We've been dating for quite some time, and we've got some good news…"

"Quite some time" turned out to be less than three months, and there was nothing whatsoever good about the news Carla shared.

Brenda listened quietly as her daughter announced how "crazy in love" she and Ben were and that they planned to marry when he got a job, which he planned to do the very next month—as soon as he was officially off parole.

Brenda was speechless as Carla, clearly in an increasingly manic state, rambled on while Ben stood by nodding in agreement, like one of those bobblehead dolls.

The girls had just been drifting off to sleep when Carla arrived, and Brenda could see their groggy confusion being slowly replaced by fear as their mother continued her high-energy proclamation of undying love for this stranger standing nearby. Appalled by the scene unfolding right in front of her, Brenda watched Carla grab Ben's hand and practically drag him over toward her daughters, who instinctively backed away as she introduced him.

"Don't be afraid, sweeties!" Carla said as she knelt in front of them and grabbed their little hands. "You're going to love Daddy-Ben! We're all going to have so much fun!

"And guess what else, girls? You're not just getting a new daddy. You're also getting a new baby brother or sister too! Isn't it just wonderful!"

Carla's euphoric announcement left Brenda speechless.

A third child, a third father—and who was this man anyway? What was Carla thinking?

Clearly, she wasn't. As Brenda watched her daughter gather up the girls and their backpacks and head out the door, she didn't see the point in correcting Carla's assessment that the tears streaming down her mother's cheeks were from joy. They were tears of utter despair.

Today, Brenda has legal custody of Tiffany and Brittany, and their baby sister, Grace, is being raised by Ben and his parents in Arkansas. Sadly, shortly after Carla gave birth to Grace, she overdosed on a lethal combination of heroin, fentanyl, and oxycodone. She was 27 years old. Brenda does her best to tell the girls good stories about their mother— pleasant stories from the times before her daughter changed, before substance abuse and mental illness turned her into a stranger.

"This isn't how I pictured my life," Brenda says. "I try not to think about what I should have done differently to help Carla. I just don't know how all of this happened…how we got here. I prayed for her all the time…What did I do wrong?"

While it's important to learn from our past, it's equally important that we don't get caught up in the guilt, anger, and self-blame that often accompanies those explorations. Most of us parented the best we could in the moment with the information we had at the time.

It's time to get better information.

A Hard Truth

When emotional and/or mental illness is part of a troubled adult child's life, we parents find it hard to know when to speak up and when to shut up. We walk a fine line as we try to determine how and when to broach subjects that need to be discussed. We are too aware that among the possible outcomes are emotional meltdowns, histrionic tantrums, and even psychotic breakdowns. Furthermore, if we have children with anger issues and character disorders, there's always the possibility of violence. The fact that some of our kids frighten us is a hard truth to admit.

Despite all the bizarre behavior and all the warning signs, there's another hard truth many well-intentioned parents have been trying to diminish or, in some cases, even deny. That truth is, these aren't just out-of-control, rebellious kids. The issue is no longer a strong-willed, button-pushing child who wants to see how far he or she can go. The truth is, many of the adult children we are desperately trying to "help" are suffering from mental and emotional illnesses that often go undiagnosed and/or untreated or—because of the stigma still attached to these labels—are frequently ignored.

Our *challenging* adult children have become *troubled* adult children, and they are fighting depression, bipolar disorder, borderline personality disorders, anxiety disorders, PTSD, and schizophrenia, to name a few. Many have been in and out of jail or prison more than once, and the ramifications of both incarceration and a criminal record have seriously impacted their ability to reintegrate into society. Let's not forget those adult children who have serious anger and denial issues, some of whom are antisocial to a psychotic and dangerous degree. Angry, bitter, and aimless, many of our adult children cannot hold jobs, and quite often their financial struggles lead to disastrous choices.

Others have been so damaged by life that they want only to end theirs. In desperation and despair, some have frequently threatened and even attempted suicide; sadly, many have succeeded.

Clearly, the consequences of the choices our troubled adult children are making have been ratcheted up through the years.

A Frightening Fact

Yet another malevolent influence threatens the lives of those we love: Countless adult children are caught up in our country's devastating epidemic of drug addiction.

Heroin, cocaine, methamphetamine, opioids, and "club drugs" have turned our children into strangers. They will do almost anything for that next high—that next fix—and nothing we say or do can break through the drugs' demonic hold on our kids.

We live in a world entirely different from the one in which most of us grew up. Today, parents around the country are barely hanging on to their sanity as they struggle to effectively help adult children who are dealing with serious, life-threatening issues due at least in part to the drug-abuse scourge bringing death and destruction to cities and towns across the country.

Unless you live on a tiny desert island off the coast of some faraway land, it's a sure bet that you know someone sucked into the quicksand of an opioid drug addiction either as a user or a seller. And it's frightening to think that more than 175 Americans *will die today* of drug overdoses.[1] And consider these numbers:

> Drug overdose is now the leading cause of death for Americans younger than 50. The Centers for Disease Control and Prevention reports that more than 64,000 Americans lost their lives to a drug overdose in 2016, including 15,446 heroin overdoses. The total is more than 20 times the number of Americans killed on 9/11.[2]

As we go to press, America's opioid epidemic is on track to claim 1 million lives by 2020,[3] with the president of the United States declaring it a "national crisis."

Of course, this combination of substance abuse, emotional and mental illnesses, and character disorders clouds our adult children's judgment—and guilt, fear, anger, unreasonable expectations, and frightening consequences cloud our own.

And if all these facts aren't enough to send us parents into rescue mode time and again, we can't forget that many of these struggling adults are responsible for the care and safety of their own children, of our grandchildren. Is it any wonder we feel the weight of responsibility on our shoulders and in our hearts? Is it any wonder we repeatedly come to our children's rescue? Is it any wonder we cry out to God, "Please help my child!"

How did we—and how did our kids—get to this point? What went wrong? We are hardworking, honest, God-fearing Christians who have always tried to do the right thing, the best thing, the most helpful thing for the children God entrusted to our care.

This isn't how life is supposed to be.

What Can We Do?

Our adult children, some of whom are seriously troubled, need professional help. But, sadly, we don't know how to make that happen—or we may be in denial about how serious their situation is. So we pay their bills, cater to their needs, bail them out, make excuses for them, and do everything possible to "help" them.

However, please hear me when I say this: *Our actions are not helping!*

The time has come for us to develop a different strategy for battle, to deploy a new arsenal of weapons, and to change our vantage point and therefore how we view not only our adult children but also our role in the relationship. We can restructure our thinking, learn effective strategies, shift our perspective, and begin to view our adult children, their challenging situations, and our responses to them in new ways—ways that just might make a difference in their lives. And in ours.

Are you ready to try?

"But, Allison, if you had any idea how hard we've tried…how many

chances we've given our child…If you only knew what life has been like for years…"

Well, folks, I do. I do know what it's like.

A Mother's Journey

When I wrote *Setting Boundaries with Your Adult Children*, my only child was serving a seven-year sentence in federal prison, of which he served five years. A great deal has happened in the years since.

While my son's heroin addiction is a thing of the past, years of IV drug abuse have affected his circulation, and a very serious motorcycle accident left him with metal pins and plates in his body. Add an unsuccessful back surgery to the equation, and he is in constant, chronic pain. Sadly, heroin has been replaced by a combination of prescription pain pills, opioids, and street drugs. Yes, addiction again.

My son has been in and out of jail and prison several times since, and the years have not been kind to him. PTSD plagues him as a result of years of substance abuse, street living, and incarceration. Sadly, painful memories of his past often bleed into his present, and separating the two is sometimes hard for him. He isolates himself from those who could truly help, and periods of depression and distorted thinking drive him deeper into the euphoric escape of drugs and criminal activity.

Like many of our troubled kids, he has above-average language skills and can masterfully manipulate a conversation—yet his social skills, decision-making ability, and coping mechanisms are below average. He is a grown man who struggles every day to survive, and my heart aches for him. After all these years, I still want him to find his purpose and live the life God has planned for him.

Yet it seems I want this for him more than he wants it for himself. And so, like many parents, I've had to learn how to let go—to love my son with open arms and trust that God is in control. I'm certainly not.

Thousands of parents have reached out to me for help over the years—generous, loving, caring, and often hopeless parents. Grasping at straws yet fearful of the truth and its consequences, they are desperate to know what to do. Many lack the resources—financial and emotional—or the knowledge of what to do. They feel alone, yet statistics prove that is not the case. There are so many of us brokenhearted parents of broken kids.

Next Steps

But when we put our hope in God, we will never be disappointed. Hope is always based on the guaranteed promises of God, and hope is something we can give to our struggling adult children. After all, "[God] helps us [parents] in all our troubles, so that we are able to help others [our adult children] who have all kinds of troubles, using the same help that we ourselves have received from God" (2 Corinthians 1:3-4 GNT).

Hope and healing can miraculously replace fear and pain when we make the transition from "This isn't how life is supposed to be" to "This is how life is. Now what does God want me to learn and do?" This transition starts when we can begin to see our troubled adult children for who they really are rather than who we *wish* they were.

For many of us, this shift in perspective is going to require genuine fortitude as we revisit some of the painful situations and circumstances that have brought us to where we are today. It's never easy to look at illnesses and issues that have caused considerable damage not only to the life of our children, but to our relationship with them as well.

Over the course of this book, we're going to talk a great deal about the issues and illnesses impacting the lives of our troubled adult children. Realize, however, that despite all this discussion about our offspring, the journey we are about to take together is ultimately about *you* and *your choices.*

It's a journey that will change your life.

And—God willing—the life of your troubled adult child.

EFFECTIVE STRATEGY

As we get started, I'd like to encourage you to keep a notepad or journal as you read through this book. From time to time, I'll suggest you jot something down for future reference. Don't worry. Your notes will be for your eyes only; you don't need to be a writer, and no one is going to grade your work.

When it comes to addressing the health and safety of our struggling children though, I've found that our emotions can sometimes get the best of us, and the physical exercise of writing can bring more clarity to our thoughts.

Chapter 2

Taking Rightful Control...of Your Home, Your Story, Your Life

Parents who love a troubled adult child live a sort of half life. We are truly ourselves only in those brief periods of time between crises—and the older our adult kids get, the shorter those periods of time become. It's like we live in a type of vacuum, watching the world go on around us, but not actually participating in it.

One of the many things that makes having a troubled adult child in our lives so hard, and that contributes to a growing isolation, is that people who have never experienced what this is like—no matter how much they want to help or support us—can never truly understand what this out-of-control living is like. With all due respect...

They have never seen their child in the throes of a psychotic break.

They don't deal with the fluctuating reality of a bipolar adult child who is manic one minute and depressed and suicidal the next.

They don't know what it's like to provide an adult child with a place to stay and a "second chance," only to find their goodwill being used and abused and their peace and safety being threatened.

They haven't been blindsided by a manipulative narcissist who will lie to your face, tell you how much she loves you, and then steal your mother's wedding ring to pawn it for drugs.

They don't know what it's like to love someone who seems to have no conscience, who doesn't care whom he hurts, and who acts out in destructive and sometimes dangerous ways.

They haven't had to be practically strip-searched in order to communicate with their child in a prison visitor room.

They can't begin to comprehend what it's like to need law enforcement to forcibly remove a noncompliant child from their home.

Or to tell their grandchildren that Mommy won't be coming home—ever.

And they can't possibly know what it's like to take out a meager life insurance policy on your adult child so you can have enough money to bury her should her actions finally catch up to her.

Loving a troubled adult child is like living in an alternative reality. We watch these things unfold in front of us, but we can't believe they're really happening. That emotional disconnect from life gets us through the situation, but it also keeps us from connecting to our children in a meaningful way.

The whole situation is an unmitigated mess.

Furthermore, it's easy to get caught up in the maelstrom of drama that so often characterizes the lives of troubled adult children. When they live with us, this close physical proximity makes it hard not to become involved. Even when they live elsewhere, they still seem to have an uncanny ability to pull us into their chaotic world. When they hurt, we hurt. During those brief periods when things are going well for them, we breathe a little easier. And when they spiral into yet another crisis, we always seem to get pulled into the funnel cloud with them. Many of us have been swept up in the chaos for so long, it seems impossible to break free.

Yet break free we must.

There is a reason the flight attendant tells parents to put on their air mask first in the event of an emergency. Sadly, a great many of us never got that wise instruction, or if we did, we ignored it. Today, we've got a nation of adult children who are breathing freely while parents are suffocating and going down for the count.

Parents, you cannot continue to allow your troubled adult children to drag you down with them. How helpful to them can you be if they exhaust your finances, drain your emotional resources, and destroy all you have worked years to develop?

Unless that's what you want.

Which, quite frankly, I don't think you do.

How do I know this? Because I know you.

And I know you because I *was* you. I *am* you.

For the longest time, you've been making choices concerning your adult children that may not always have been helpful. You've been caught up in responding to their problems in ways that haven't always been healthy for you—or them. You've neglected to take healthy control when and where it was most needed.

Why is that?

I would hazard to guess there is a one-word answer: fear.

Please Help!

> *I live with two adult sons who have a difficult time holding jobs, spend hours in bed while I am at work, are disrespectful, and become violent with me. They are angry with their father because he left them when they were young. They are up all night smoking pot and refusing to follow any of my rules. I have had to call the police on my own sons on many occasions, and now I am trying to make the difficult decision of having them both evicted and then having to deal with all the consequences of that decision. I am so exhausted from them. What do I do?*

> *I am a Christian, but my life is out of control. I have a failed marriage. I am single parenting my children, and my oldest has been diagnosed with ADHD. The father is not in the picture at present. My older son is hard to handle: He is not behaving well, to say the least, and he disrespects me. He pushes all my buttons, and I end up becoming dysfunctional around him. I am worried I may be setting up patterns that will not serve him well in the future.*

> *Our 20-year-old son called and asked to come home. He has been verbally abusive and violent. He has used drugs, stolen*

from us, stayed up all night, regularly gone to work late, and gotten laid off. When we set some boundaries, he chose to leave. Now, two months later, he wants to come back home and will agree to anything we say he must do. In his words, "Anything is better than being homeless." Should we invite him back?

These stories—and more like them—came to me from readers asking for advice about how to move forward. Because I don't know the full story, I can't make any specific recommendations. I can, however, share what I feel in my heart as I read their desperate pleas...

Parents, please wake up!

In all these cases, what we parents desperately need to do, but seem to fear, is to take control.

When Did We Become So Passive?

First, being in control is not the same as being controlling. Controlling people impose their beliefs on others and tend to judge others by arbitrary rules they deem as universal. But being "in control" is something entirely different. Our children may call us controlling as we try to regain the healthy control we have lost, but that is because this is new behavior for us and for them.

But your child is an adult, responsible for his or her own actions. Regardless of the mistakes you've made, you are not to blame if your child is a drug addict, an alcoholic, or a chronic gambler. And you certainly aren't to blame if you are being verbally abused by your child. After all, you can't control your child's actions, nor should you try—that would be controlling.

But you *can* control your response to those actions.

You can learn to say *no* with firm conviction and *yes* with honest authenticity. You can open your mouth and tell your child, "I love you, but this must stop. You do not have authority over me or this household."

Understanding that you can control your responses to your child's actions will help you be willing to take a stand and to set healthy boundaries. Gaining control of your responses, though, is not a passive exercise: It takes involvement, commitment, and the willingness to be loving but firm. Being in control of our responses to our children also requires the ability to identify where we need to change and the recognition that we need to actively pursue that change.

Choosing healthy, God-honoring control is one of those monumental decisions that can change the course of your life.

You Tell the Story

A popular phrase—widely embraced in media, business, and political outlets these days—is "controlling the narrative." That is, telling the story your way before someone else tells it—and possibly tells it more convincingly—their way. Hold on to that thought for a minute.

So many factors have made us who we are today. The sad truth is, many of us have been so busy responding to chaos, reacting to situations, and running on the gerbil wheel of insanity that we haven't considered what—or who—is controlling us and thereby writing our story for us. For the longest time, for instance, I allowed my son's heroin addiction and his poor choices to control my life. I identified the problem, and I thought it was my son and his issues. I believed that everything in my life would be fine if only he would change. Yes, he needed to change. But so did I. Big time. I needed to start telling my own stories.

And an important theme in my story needed to be controlling how I respond to the turmoil in my life. We all know there is actually very little we can truly control in life—particularly the situations and circumstances that arise in the chaotic life of someone battling an addiction or mental illness. But we can control—and we need to control—how we respond to that chaos. We can choose whether to call ourselves victims or survivors. And in the event we allow our troubled adult children to live with us, we can most certainly control the conditions under which this invitation is extended. Quite simply, while we want the experience to be as truly helpful for our children as possible, the fact remains that this is our home, and we have accepted a great deal of financial responsibility to create a safe haven for all who live here.

In other words, our home, our rules.

When we control the narrative and lay down the rules for living in our home, we take a step toward control, and with that step, we are beginning to change our stories. With God's help, our wholehearted commitment to being healthy, and the right tools, we can let go of our fears—*What happens if I kick him out? What happens if I don't send her this check?*—and trust God with the outcome.

And this healthy move in the right direction starts with our thoughts.

The Battlefield in Your Brain

In his book *30 Days to Overcoming Emotional Strongholds,* Tony Evans shows how destructive negative thoughts and emotions can be, and he provides a strategy for taking control of them:

> One of Satan's favorite strategies is to plant his thoughts in our minds, disguising them as our own thoughts. We accept them as true and begin to act on them. This is the same strategy he used with Eve in the garden when he twisted God's truth and enticed her to sin.
>
> But if Satan is responsible for these sinful thoughts, how can we be blamed for thinking them or acting on them? The answer is that you and I are responsible for what we do with these thoughts once they enter our minds...
>
> When a thought enters your mind, luring you into an emotional stronghold of worry, doubt, anger, hate, or shame, you have two choices. You can *reject* the thought, or you can *adopt* it and make it your own. By rejecting it, you tear down the stronghold and put an end to the false way of thinking. It can't dominate or corrupt your emotions any longer.[1]

Think about your present situation. Surely it's not a new set of circumstances. I'm guessing you've been on that out-of-control gerbil wheel for a while, and nothing has worked. Maybe it's time to change your thoughts. Maybe it's time to tell a new story.

Simply put—and as you've heard me say—maybe it's time to take back the control you've lost in your home.

Serenity and SANITY

If you've read any of the books in the Setting Boundaries® series, you've read a prayer that I've included in every book. "The Serenity Prayer" is the common name for an originally untitled prayer by the theologian Reinhold Niebuhr. A prayer about learning how to accept, it has been adopted by Alcoholics Anonymous and other 12-step programs. Chances are you've heard all or part of this well-known prayer. It's a long prayer, but this is the part quoted most often: "God, grant me the serenity to accept the things I cannot change [control], courage to change [control] the things I can, and wisdom to know the difference."[2]

Control what you can, and be kind to yourself about what you can't.

Now that you're ready to take healthy control, it's time to learn how. Next, we'll journey together through six steps that can help you navigate uncharted territory and change your life.

EFFECTIVE STRATEGY

Begin to reframe your thinking insofar as control. Prayerfully consider what's within your area of control and what's beyond your control. Do you need to exhibit more healthy control or be less judgmentally controlling? Be honest with yourself. Grab your journal and write down your thoughts on this hot-button topic.

Chapter 3

SANITY Strategies

Stop, Assemble, Nip, Implement, Trust, Yield

Well-meaning believers who don't quite grasp what we're going through with our troubled adult kids will often try to comfort us with words such as "Trust God; He's in control." While these friends have good intentions and a sincere desire to bring comfort, I'm not convinced that Christian platitudes are what we desperately need at moments of crisis.

If the solution to the serious and sometimes life-threatening problems we face with troubled adult children—who are addicted to drugs, who are mentally ill, and who are in many cases completely void of character and integrity—is merely to pray harder, surrender more to Jesus, and let go and let God, then why aren't our kids healed?

Telling a mother who wakes up to find her daughter dead on the sofa from a drug overdose to just trust in God's plan somehow seems more than a little cold, more than a little disconnected from the tragic reality. Or to tell the father who discovers his son has been forging his name on checks and depleted all but $100 from his retirement account to "Just give it over to the Lord" is, I believe, not what he really needs at that moment.

What do we parents need when life is so not what we expected and our hearts are more broken than we ever thought possible? Well,

Alcoholics Anonymous has twelve steps, Celebrate Recovery has eight steps, and I want to offer us struggling parents six steps to SANITY. These steps are effective tools you can use confidently before, during, and after any crisis with your troubled adult child.

Why SANITY?

As I mentioned earlier, my son, Chris, was in prison when I wrote *Setting Boundaries with Your Adult Children*. That book was born out of years of pain that I had poured out onto the hundreds of pages of a half-dozen spiral-top steno pads.

Many of those notes were my desperate cries to God, begging for His divine intervention in my son's life. If you're a parent in pain, you know exactly how those prayers go: "Lord, heal my son. Jesus, save my daughter. Father God, please tell me what to do. I can't take this anymore!"

In the midst of a particularly bad season when my son was in a psychiatric hospital on a mandatory 72-hour hold, I wrote this in my journal: "Lord, when will this insanity stop? I feel like a gerbil, running as fast as I can on the wheel of life but going nowhere."

It was then, after years of my unintentional but crippling enabling, that I was finally able to see the light. God convicted me with this painful truth: *Allison, you are handicapping Chris, not helping him. You have to stop repeating this pattern!*

That was the first Holy Spirit prompt I received years ago: *Stop.* A small word for such a big step.

My own messed-up past and my own personal issues made it very hard for me not only to set healthy boundaries but also to communicate with my son in ways that fostered trust and built a healthy connection that would survive the tough times. Yes, my love for Chris was strong, but in many ways, it was suffocating him. At the same time, my love for Chris fed my own brokenness—and that's the essence of codependency: the excessive emotional or psychological reliance on a partner, typically a partner who requires support due to an illness or addiction. I had to stop coming to his rescue.

There was much I had to stop in those early days with my son because I was living out the well-known definition of insanity: repeating the same behavior and expecting different results. It took me a while, but I was eventually able to jump off that gerbil wheel by following six steps the Lord placed on my heart. These six steps helped me become less controlling and gain healthy control of my life and acquire a deeper understanding of God's plan and purpose for me. And the first letter of each of these six steps just happened (!) to spell the word *SANITY*. I believe these steps can be effective strategies for our efforts to connect with our troubled adult children.

These steps toward SANITY depend on our changing how we see our relationships with our children. We need to see the relationship and our child as they really are. This adjustment to reality will bring a great deal of pain to both parties. And our finally taking control of the situation will have us wading into a murky pool of emotions that sometimes makes it difficult to think rationally.

But the SANITY steps will help you think more clearly even as you acknowledge and process your emotions. These six steps will also help you see your way forward to a new future.

Stop your enabling behaviors and poor choices.

Assemble supportive people.

Nip excuses in the bud.

Implement a plan of action.

Trust the voice of the Spirit.

Yield everything to God.

Stop Your Enabling Behaviors and Poor Choices

They say the first step in any journey is often the hardest, and that's true here. This first of the six steps to SANITY sounds like the easiest, yet it will be one of the most difficult. At the same time, however, this first step can bring a level of illumination to your life that will enable you to see more clearly than you have for years. The *S* step in SANITY will also set the course for all the steps that follow—and those steps can be done in any order. But the *S* step does need to be first.

And once we finally decide to STOP all the enabling behaviors and poor choices that allow our adult children to continue their destructive patterns, that will be the end of our doing what we've always done but expecting different results. God willing, we will feel deep conviction in our souls to make choices that will change our lives—and theirs.

Simply put, when we stop, the healing starts. And that's a promise.

Question: What do you feel God is telling you to stop? List everything that comes to mind. Take some time to think and listen. Don't hold anything back. When your list is complete, rank order these steps starting with your top priority.

Assemble Supportive People

Nowhere in Scripture is the importance of traveling through life together more beautifully depicted than in Ecclesiastes 4:9-12:

> Two are better off than one, because together they can work more effectively. If one of them falls down, the other can help him up. But if someone is alone and falls, it's just too bad, because there is no one to help him. If it is cold, two can sleep together and stay warm, but how can you keep warm by yourself? Two people can resist an attack that would defeat one person alone. A rope made of three cords is hard to break (GNT).

It's easy to isolate ourselves when we have adult children struggling with serious substance abuse issues or mental illness. But knowing we aren't alone is important. Whenever life gets tough, every single one of us needs people nearby who can encourage us by listening, praying, and offering godly counsel as well as a shoulder to lean on. It's vital that you surround yourself with supportive people you trust, people who can listen with love, give you biblical advice, and help you navigate confusing and painful situations. We can no longer let ourselves hide behind guilt, shame, or pride.

We parents know that when our troubled adult children are in the throes of drug addiction or suffering from brain-related illnesses, a supportive treatment team is critical. This treatment team can consist of psychologists, psychiatrists, physicians, counselors, therapists, social workers, patient advocates, and even lawyers. We parents need our own treatment team comprised of friends, family, church members, professionals, counselors, and good old-fashioned prayer warriors. We must be willing to ask for help, pour out our pain, and allow God to work His miracles through the people He has placed in our lives.

At first your support may be a single person, and that's okay. And it doesn't matter whether that person is a family member, a friend, a pastor, a licensed Christian counselor, or a circle of strangers in a reputable support group. You just need to start *somewhere*.

A word of caution, though: Make sure your support person or team shares your Christian values, is able to listen with love and understanding, and offers sound biblical advice. Receiving advice from someone who doesn't share your faith can lead to confusion, frustration, and greater pain. Additionally, receiving advice from someone who doesn't understand your specific issue, or who isn't aware of the psychological, emotional, or physical ramifications of what they are saying to you, can lead to worse suffering. Ask God to direct you to the supportive people He wants you to assemble so you have help when life's storms hit.

God may direct you to an already existing support group for people who are in pretty much the same situation you're in. In most communities, for instance, it's easy to find groups for people dealing with divorce, single parenting, unemployment, financial problems, codependency, parental enabling, health concerns, addictions, depression, or other matters. Check with area churches, community centers, and nonprofit organizations. Conduct an online search, too, but exercise prayerful caution when divulging personal information to anyone online.

Because the associated contact information of resources frequently changes, I've decided to provide pertinent information on my website where updates can be made frequently. Visit my website at Allison Bottke.com for current resources.

Question: Who will you reach out to today to ask for help or support?

Nip Excuses in the Bud

He's a good kid. All his problems are because of those friends he made in high school. It's all their fault.

She struggled so much as a child. If her teachers had just been more patient with her...

Setting healthy boundaries in any area of life can be fraught with obstacles. Quite often, those obstacles are excuses—both those we tell ourselves and those other people tell us.

Being able to apply the *N* step and NIP excuses in the bud—to keep them from becoming a foundational element in our narrative that hinders our movement toward SANITY—depends first on our ability to identify excuses as excuses. This can be difficult, so don't be surprised if this step takes you some time to master. Having come up with so many different excuses for why our children are in bondage to their issues, we can find it hard to separate truth from fiction. Yet, it *can* be done. And it needs to be done because real healing and restoration begin when we stop believing lies and excuses. Many valid explanations for our children's issues may exist, but in almost every case, that explanation does not exempt them from accepting responsibility for their choices.

Question: What excuses have you made for your child? In what ways have these excuses kept both of you stuck? Be specific.

Implement a Plan of Action

First John 3:18 is a convicting call for parents of troubled adult children: "Let us not love with words or speech but with actions and in truth." It's not too late to start establishing healthy boundaries and taking healthy control of your life that is being significantly impacted by your children. Create an action plan that clearly identifies boundaries and the consequences for the one who breaches them. As we seek to restore a relationship that has been damaged by poor boundaries, our number-one priority is to remain lovingly firm in our resolve to change.

Also, an action plan becomes a much more powerful tool when you put it down on paper. Writing out your plan adds strength and clarity to your resolve. It also communicates to your children that you are serious about these changes.

It's a landmark moment when you begin to dig yourself out from under the toxic emotional trash that has been burying you alive, when you calmly and rationally set forth—aloud or on paper—the steps you are going to take toward health.

The intensity of your need to develop and implement a plan of action is largely dependent on the degree of your child's dependence on you. Does your adult son, for instance, live with you and depend entirely on you for his support? Does your daughter have her own apartment but depends on you to help pay for utilities and provide free babysitting? Have you given your child a place to dry out and get clean because he can't afford an inpatient treatment center? Perhaps you have a child who is addicted to hi-tech gadgets and fancy cars but often can't make the payments and comes to you for cash.

Or perhaps the dependence doesn't involve money. I know a parent whose son and his girlfriend lived in an apartment, but they had several cars, a boat, a motorcycle, and a dozen or so very large plastic storage bins filled with heaven knows what, and they depended on her garage, driveway, basement, and attic to store everything. She parked on the street while his things were safe and dry. When she finally decided to stop the insanity and take control, she developed an action plan that outlined stages for him to remove his property—and consequences if he didn't. It was a very fair plan, designed to take place over several months. The first step was removing the boat in her driveway. He was livid, but she was calm. It was time. She had parked on the street for five years. During that first winter when she could pull into her own garage, her support group filled it with balloons. When the automatic garage door opened, she was greeted by her friends—the people who had helped her take control in a healthy way.

Parents of troubled adult children also need to take control of their homes in a healthy way. These parents need to develop and implement a plan of action when their adult child is living in their house and the situation is becoming untenable. Equally important is a plan of action when parents are considering opening their home to a troubled adult child. Because this situation has such great potential for further conflict and pain, a written plan is absolutely necessary. I've devoted chapter 15 to this topic: "When Your Troubled Adult Child Lives with You." This might be hard for you to read, especially if Holy Spirit conviction is working in your heart and head to help you clearly see reality.

Question: What current situation related to your adult child is becoming untenable? What is the goal of the plan of action you need to develop? Jot down any thoughts about that action plan.

Trust the Voice of the Spirit

Isaiah 30:21 sets forth a beautiful promise for believers: "Whether you turn to the right or to the left, your ears will hear a voice behind you, saying, 'This is the way; walk in it.'" That voice—described as "still small" elsewhere (1 Kings 19:12 NKJV) and called "intuition" by some—is a powerful teacher if we don't ignore it.

When we parents do ignore God's voice or our own intuition—when we don't let ourselves see reality for what it is—we do so at our own risk and at the further risk of our troubled adult children. We parents often know in our gut when things aren't right. That inner voice speaks to our hearts about a specific situation or issue. How do we respond? Too frequently we ignore the voice and dismiss the instinct. As one parent wrote, "I saw the signs—late nights, sleeping in, irritability, weight loss, that 'look' in his eyes. I just didn't want to admit that my son had a serious problem."

In no situation do we need to trust our instincts more than when we suspect our adult children are on drugs, have alcohol problems, or are involved in illegal activity. When that shrill sixth-sense alarm goes off in our hearts and souls, we need to take heed. It's a warning many of us have ignored for too long.

But let me add a gentle word of caution here, fellow parents. Please don't beat yourselves up for missing the cues or ignoring your conscience. Extend yourself grace, ask forgiveness, and move forward in confidence.

Heeding that sixth sense—paying attention when we hear God's still, small voice—is also crucial when we decide we are ready to try to restore trust with a loved one who has hurt us. When we hear the Lord's voice, we must trust the messages He places on our hearts and in our minds. God can *lead* us or sometimes *restrain* us in our decision-making process. We need to learn to rely more on God and less on ourselves as we more consistently ask Him to reveal truth to our *hearts* and *minds* through the voice of the Spirit. When He does, we need to then trust that truth.

Only rarely, however, do we hear God's voice the way we hear a family member's or a friend's. God usually speaks to us in one of two ways: through prompting and through teaching. *Promptings* are those inspired ideas and inner nudges to do something with or for a certain person at a certain time. *Teachings* from sermons, talks, or books help us respond properly in specific situations, they provide clarification, and they coach us in our attitude adjustment. In short, promptings tend to enhance our spiritual intuition, and teachings help us develop and refine our spiritual perspective on life events.

Our spiritual intuition as well as our sensitivity to God's presence and voice are helped when we maintain a running dialogue with God through our waking hours. Doing so—speaking to Him and listening for His guidance—requires discipline. With practice, we will more naturally recognize and respond to this spiritual intuition. Also helping us recognize God's voice is our study of His Word. God speaks to us through the Bible, and using the truths on those pages, the Holy Spirit reveals to us more about God, His purposes, and His ways. Consider this truth from Henry Blackaby and Claude King's book *Experiencing God*:

> Our experiences alone cannot be our guide. Every experience must be controlled and understood by the Scriptures. The God revealed in Scripture does not change. Throughout your life, you will have times when you want to respond based on your experiences or your wisdom. Seeking to know God's will based on circumstances alone can be misleading. This should be your guideline: Always

go back to the Bible for truth (or for the Holy Spirit to reveal truth).[1]

We need to be sure that any action we are considering lines up with what the Lord teaches in Scripture. As we learn to recognize and be confident that we have heard God's voice, we also need to be sure that what we think we are hearing is consistent with what we know of God's character, His will, and His ways. Blackaby and King add this:

> God speaks to individuals, and He can do it in any way He pleases. As you walk in an intimate love relationship with God, you will come to recognize His voice. You will know when God is speaking to you. He will see to it.[2]

Of course, God will be sure we hear His voice. That's what He wants for us too.

Now, this idea of hearing God's voice as you read Scripture may be new to you. If so, start simply. Choose a short reading from the Bible. Read a psalm or perhaps two. Then let those words lead you into praying about your situation. Thank God for what He is already doing in your life and in the life of your son or daughter…Give Him your negative thoughts and painful memories…and ask Him to transform your thinking…Then ask Him to open the eyes of your heart and mind… and to lead you to a deeper understanding of what He wants you to do in response to the needs of your troubled adult child.

Once you ask, spend some time listening for God's direction. His guidance may even come from the very words you just read in the Bible. If you think you've heard from God but you're not sure, share your thoughts with a trusted member of your support team who also knows God well and is a student of the Word.

In addition, know that God's voice in His Word is truth that guides: "The unfolding of your words gives light; it gives understanding to the simple" (Psalm 119:130). You can be confident that God does indeed lead His people through His Word.

When we listen to and follow the Spirit's voice of truth and wisdom, and when, in His power, we conquer the demons of habitually poor choices and responses, we can celebrate a true victory.

Question: When, if ever, have you experienced the Holy Spirit guiding your response to your child's behavior, attitudes, or words? Explain why you did or didn't act according to the Spirit's leading. Whether you did or didn't follow that guidance, describe what happened.

Yield Everything to God

Letting go of our mental and emotional junk—yielding all we are to God—allows Him to cleanse us, heal us, free us, and transform us. As I wrote in *Setting Boundaries with Your Adult Children,* our true healing begins when we realize in our hearts as well as in our heads that we must "let go and let God" concerning all things, not just the painful situations concerning our adult children. This kind of surrender doesn't mean we are giving up or that we no longer care about what happens to our adult children. On the contrary, our surrender means we are relinquishing them to a far greater and infinitely more powerful Caregiver.[3]

At some point, every Christian who truly wants to walk in God's will is going to have to release his or her problems to God and choose to trust Him for whatever happens. This yielding, however, is not a sign of defeat or weakness. In fact, it is quite the opposite. Yielding ourselves brings us closer to God, increasing our dependence on Him, our desire to obey His will, and our knowledge of Jesus's character and His ways.

When thoughts of our children consume our waking hours and threaten to drag us down into the pit of despair, knowing the character of Christ means knowing how to respond to our children and to their/our circumstances. Consider the life of Jesus. If anyone had cause to respond negatively to painful experiences and extreme adversity, it was Jesus. He experienced the greatest suffering that ever took place; He endured unimaginable anguish and torment, both physical and spiritual. Yet throughout His life and even on the cross, Jesus consistently exhibited love, forgiveness, compassion, kindness, endurance, humility, submission, holiness, righteousness, and purity. Such characteristics distinguished Him as the selfless, sacrificial Lamb of God, who was more concerned about others than about Himself.

When we make our relationship with Jesus first and foremost in our lives, we grow in our ability to—among other things—love, forgive, show compassion, be kind, endure tough times, live with humility, and choose purity. As we get to know Jesus better, we also move toward spiritual maturity and, with it, inner freedom from suffocating fear and debilitating guilt. Remember what God promises us: "Don't be afraid, for I am with you. Don't be discouraged, for I am your God. I will strengthen you and help you. I will hold you up with my victorious right hand" (Isaiah 41:10 NLT). The Holy Spirit does exactly that for us.

Question: Describe a time when you yielded to God someone or something very dear to you. What happened circumstantially? Probably more important, what happened within you? What is God calling you to yield to Him today? Why are you or aren't you reluctant to do so?

The Strength of SANITY

Loving our kids with open arms means so much more than simply letting go of them. Loving our kids means letting them live their lives while we begin to again live our own. But what would our lives look like if our days were not being determined by rescuing, fixing, controlling, or worrying about the consequences of the choices our kids are making? Can you even imagine?

These six steps toward SANITY can help you both imagine that kind of existence and help you get there. Again—and I can't emphasize this enough—we find peace and SANITY as we intentionally develop our faith in God and our relationship with the Father, the Son, and the Holy Spirit. Our challenging life experiences encourage us to rely on God: "The LORD gives strength to his people" (Psalm 29:11). God will give us the strength and the SANITY we need to live a life that honors and glorifies Him.

So, if mental illness and substance abuse are holding our adult children hostage, and we really want to help them before they kill themselves or someone else, we must learn effective strategies that will encourage them to want to help themselves—inasmuch as they are able to do so. Applying the SANITY steps—and perhaps sharing the

SANITY steps with your adult kids—is something you can start doing right now.

In fact, at any time, you can jump off the gerbil wheel of insanity—and into the embrace of a loving Father who will never forsake you.

EFFECTIVE STRATEGY

Grab your notebook and, first, ask God to show you what you need to STOP (the *S*). Take some time to think about why you let those enabling behaviors take over your life. What issue or wish do you think was at the root of those behaviors? Ask God to give you freedom from whatever has fueled your enabling actions.

Then ask the Lord to make it clear to you which SANITY step He wants you to focus on next.

Chapter 4

Experiencing Spiritual Growth and Establishing Healthy Boundaries

Establishing and then living according to healthy personal, physical, psychological, and spiritual boundaries allows us to lead safe and God-honoring lives. But learning how to live this way isn't a quick or simple process; we develop strong boundaries over the course of our lives as we grow and learn.

As parents of troubled adult children, we desperately want them to grow and learn as well, yet that doesn't seem to be happening. At least not that we can see or as fast as we wish it would.

However—and this is where some of us get stuck—it's not just our children who need to keep learning and growing. Just because we're the grown-ups doesn't mean we have all the answers. And just because we're God-fearing Christians praying fervently for our kids doesn't mean we are walking with God and in His will the way we could be.

However much we miss the mark, the fact is, it's our faith in God and the hope for a miraculous intervention in our child's life that gives many of us the strength to keep going. So we immerse ourselves in Bible study, prayer, and daily devotionals—waiting (not always patiently) for God to provide a solution to our dilemma. I have some other suggestions as well. Keep reading.

Break the Chain of Dependence

Many of us who are parents of troubled adult children find our lives revolving around a very real—and very sick—dysfunctional dependence that is keeping us and our children from personal growth.

Our kids, for instance, depend on us to soften the consequences of their actions or inaction. They depend on our time and our money. They depend on us to turn the other cheek to their harsh and hurtful words, yet open our hearts, our wallets, and the door to our home. They depend on us to accept their elaborate excuses for their wrongdoing, and sometimes they even ask us to make up our own excuses for them. They depend on us to protect them and sometimes their children as well.

In return, we depend on their needing us to be their anchor, their safe port in the storm, their savior. We depend on them to validate our worth. (So many of us desperately need to be needed.) And when everything goes south, as it so often does, we aren't surprised to be disappointed yet again by their behavior and its consequences. At that point, we take on the blame for trusting, believing, and hoping once again: "How could I be so foolish?"

Stop! Such dysfunctional dependence only keeps us running on the gerbil wheel of insanity, getting us absolutely nowhere.

Stop. Remember the *S* step.

When we end this dance of dysfunctional dependence with our children, and we instead start to depend more fully on God and His wisdom provided in the Word, the chains of our bondage to codependency begin to fall away.

A Sad Reality

Many of our adult kids have traveled far away from God, if they ever truly knew Him in the first place. They don't trust God or call out to Him except perhaps when they are in trouble and desperate. Even then, their ideas about who God is and how He provides may be quite skewed.

It's probably safe to say that most of our children are also not connected to the indwelling Christ whose character we believers are called to reflect. Our adult children are not aware of, responsive to, or dependent on Jesus as a daily part of their life. And they have no desire to learn what His Word says about how they are to live.

Sadly, many of them say to us, "I don't believe in your God. If there were a God, life wouldn't be so hard. What kind of God makes someone go through all this pain and anguish?"

Although there's no denying that their struggles are real, I'm not convinced they are really "going through" anything. For the most part—and I mean no disrespect because I've been there myself—you've been going through it for them. (More on that to come!)

Pushing Through Pain

Athletes frequently talk about their need to push through the pain, referring to either the standard training their sport requires or the hard work of rehabilitation after an injury. By pushing through the pain, these athletes grow stronger—and, yes, we have a metaphor for life. You've probably heard, "The only way out of something is to go through it." The statement isn't exactly true, though. There's actually another way out of something, and that is to back up, turn around, and retreat.

While there are times in life when retreat is a wise choice, it shouldn't be the default for anyone. Habitually avoiding trials, tribulation, and pain of any kind can have a decidedly negative effect on us and truly stunt our growth. Besides, we might be trying to avoid an experience that God wants to use to teach us a valuable life lesson.

You see, it's in the process of "going through something"—where we do some much-needed spiritual work—that deep growth happens. What we learn during that process determines how we come out on the other side. How will we ever know what is on the other side if we don't go through those hard times?

Sadly, a lot of 20-, 30-, 40-, and even 50-year-old kids seldom get to the other side of anything, much less learn the critical character-forming life lessons available along the way. Instead, they've learned to back up, turn around, and retreat. Many of our offspring have also learned that drugs can numb pain, fear, or anger, and can justify any action, and Mom, Dad, Grandpa, Grandma, or a sibling will be there to pick up the pieces so they don't have to.

Owning Our Own Issues

Our lives cannot be based on the hope that our children will eventually have a spiritual epiphany and finally see the light. Instead, we must see our own light and base our lives on loving God and following Jesus's example.

And much of what we have done for our children is what Jesus would do. Forgiving is good. Helping is good. Being there for our adult children is good. But when living in constant need, crisis, or trouble has become the rule and not the exception for our adult children, it's time for us to step back and take a look at our lives. We must recognize our own weaknesses as well as our unhelpful behaviors that enable our children's unhealthy actions and decisions. Then we must make the changes in our own patterns of behavior—changes that only we can make.

Key to making those healthy changes in behavior is becoming aware of what's really going on inside our heads and our hearts. But learning to pay attention to what we're thinking, what we're feeling, and why we have those thoughts and emotions can be a daunting challenge. Often, when our own issues are—at their core—unhealthy boundaries, we have developed a keen ability to shift the focus off of us and onto others. We do that because we find it too painful to look at our own stuff. So, we stay stuck.

Keeping Safe

During the first 35 years of my life, I was relatively clueless about boundaries. Of course, I knew the word, but like a lot of folks, I associated it primarily with real estate—as in fences, property lines, or lot lines. It wasn't until I got to know Jesus and began to really process my mess of a life in counseling that I learned life is all about boundaries—good and bad, healthy and unhealthy, honored and violated.

Those of us raised in dysfunctional families—or in families where feelings and emotions weren't regularly discussed—have probably had little experience with healthy boundaries. Therefore, coming to understand boundaries and then learning how to establish them will be important to our personal growth and spiritual development.

To grow in these ways, however, we must identify and choose to respect our own rights and needs; become assertive and skilled at taking care of ourselves in relationships; and overcome things like low self-esteem, passivity, fear, aggressiveness, negative thoughts, and painful memories. Doing so will allow your true self to emerge, and suddenly healthy boundaries—particularly healthy psychological boundaries—become the fences that protect your heart and mind and keep you safe. That kind of safety may be something you have never before experienced, which might explain why those of us trying (usually unsuccessfully) to rescue our adult kids and keep them safe usually fail.

If we parents have difficulty setting healthy boundaries and communicating our needs and wants, is it a surprise when our adult children also struggle in these areas?

Healthy boundaries define who we are and influence all areas of our lives. In fact, as we establish spiritual boundaries, we—and our children—can learn critical life lessons. At this point, though, the student is you. Not your offspring. Not your spouse. Not other family members or your friends. You.

Spiritual Boundaries

How can we set healthy boundaries, replace destructive habits, and undo damage that's been done to our spirits? How can our lives come to be characterized by compassion, mercy, justice, and love when these feelings and traits are often buried deep under emotional pain and heartache?

Quite simply, we can't. We can't make these radical changes on our own. Our human limitations prevent that. Only with God's help—only with His Spirit's transforming work—can we receive a new nature. Only by reorganizing our priorities, putting God first, understanding our identity in Christ, and making time for fundamental spiritual disciplines like prayer and Bible study can our lives begin to reflect the character of Christ.

In their book *How People Grow,* Drs. Henry Cloud and John Townsend explained the necessity of spiritual growth this way:

> When people came to us for counseling, we wanted them to understand that the issues they were working on were not growth issues or counseling issues, but spiritual growth issues. Spiritual growth, in our mind, was the answer to everything...Spiritual growth should affect relationship problems, emotional problems, and all other problems of life. There is no such thing as our "spiritual life" and then our "real life." It is all one.
>
> ...We wanted people who were growing to know not only how to grow, but that their growth was biblical growth. We wanted them to understand that "if you are getting better, it is because you are growing spiritually. You are doing what the Bible says to do." People need not only to grow, but also to understand where that growth fits into a larger picture of God's plan for them and his plan of redemption. It is good to know that their growth is for him.[1]

Maintaining healthy spiritual boundaries is an integral part of spiritual growth and walking in obedience to God. That's why constructing boundaries around our relationship with God is healthy. These boundaries protect our daily time with the Lord—time that we spend reading the Word, praying, praising, and worshipping God—time that He uses to make us more like Jesus.

I'm not sure I would have survived these six decades were it not for my relationship with God and the wisdom and guidance He pours into my parched soul on a daily basis through His Word and His Spirit. Learning to view my journey through a lens of faith in Almighty God truly saved my life.

Sadly, many of our children are not viewing life through a lens of faith. Or if they are, their perspective is often distorted by a skewed perception of who God is and how He works to grow us and shape our character. Learning to reorganize their priorities, put God first, understand their identity in Christ, and make time for prayer and Bible study are spiritual disciplines our children desperately need to incorporate in their lives, yet we cannot force them to act.

If we want to make a difference and connect with our troubled kids in a way that just might, over time, plant a seed or light a spark in their bruised, broken, and sometimes blackened hearts, these kids need to see the face of God. After all, who knows more about pain than Jesus? Our kids need to experience the character of Christ and witness the fruit that comes when people live with the Holy Spirit as their strength and their guide.

"Well, that sounds great, Allison," you might say, "but who exactly is this saintly instructor, this spiritual role model?"

In a word? *You.*

It's time to stop telling our kids why they need Jesus and instead show them Jesus. Consistently. We show them by being parents who walk the talk. Parents who celebrate the freedom that comes with godly control of our actions and a willingness to accept the consequences of our wrong choices. Parents who don't always have all the answers but are connected to and dependent on Jesus as a daily part of life. Parents who are willing to go through whatever pain life might bring and ask God, "What do You want me to learn from this?" And parents who understand that God grows us through pain and that when we learn the biblical lesson He has for us, we come out on the other side a changed—and better—person.

Why We Need Boundaries

Before I go any further, it's important to know what a boundary is and what it is not. This may seem like basic information, but it's important that you clear out any misconceptions or lies you might believe about them. Maybe you believe that it's selfish to say no or that you're rejecting your children when you refuse to loan them money. Satan has successfully told us lies about boundaries and, in doing so, has kept us in bondage to misconceptions about responsibility, accountability, and consequences—critical aspects of our ability to effectively connect with our children. Consider these truths about boundaries:

A Boundary Is:	A Boundary Is Not:
Healthy	Rejection
Necessary	Selfish
Biblical	Sinful
Respectful	Disrespectful
Loving	Dishonoring

I like the way Dr. Henry Cloud and Dr. John Townsend clarify this concept in their seminal book *Boundaries*:

> Any confusion of responsibility and ownership in our lives is a problem of *boundaries*. Just as homeowners set physical property lines around their land, we need to set mental, physical, emotional, and spiritual boundaries for our lives to help us distinguish what our responsibility is and what it isn't…The inability to set appropriate boundaries at appropriate times with the appropriate people can be very destructive.
>
> And this is one of the most serious problems facing Christians today. Many sincere, dedicated believers struggle with tremendous confusion about when it is biblically appropriate to set limits.[2]

Understanding why we need boundaries in the first place will not only help us make healthy choices; it will also change our lives—and perhaps, through our example, the lives of our children.

Today's free fall of emotional insanity is not God's plan. He wants us to live with boundaries. In fact, we need boundaries simply because God has mandated it, and He set the first boundary in the Garden of Eden:

> The LORD God took the man and put him in the Garden of Eden to work it and take care of it. And the LORD God commanded the man, "You are free to eat from any tree in the garden; but you must not eat from the tree of the knowledge of good and evil, for when you eat from it you will certainly die" (Genesis 2:15-17).

As we know, the violation of this boundary had catastrophic consequences. When Adam and Eve disrespected the boundary God had set, He sent them out of Eden and away from His presence.

God's commandments are additional boundaries He has established for us. The world would like us to think of these boundaries as harsh, judgmental, or restrictive. The world goes on to say that many of God's laws are no longer applicable in our modern times and should be interpreted more broadly.

But God established these commandments—these boundaries—for our good, and adhering to them helps us withstand enormous pain and pressure. Deuteronomy 10:12-13 asks this question:

> What does the LORD your God require of you, but to fear the LORD your God, to walk in all his ways, to love him, to serve the LORD your God with all your heart and with all your soul, and to keep the commandments and statutes of the LORD, which I am commanding you today *for your good?* (ESV, emphasis added).

Let the wisdom of God's Word change you from the inside out. Every day, make time to read, study, and meditate on passages from the Bible. Ask God to give you the wisdom you need to understand and then to apply its principles to the situations you're facing. The more you learn about applying biblical wisdom to your life, the better you'll be able to set healthy boundaries and the more easily you'll be able to live according to God's will for you.

God has designed the freedom-producing boundaries found throughout the Bible for our good. Following His plan helps us not only survive, but thrive.

Jesus Had Boundaries

As we learn to walk in God's will and respect the boundaries He has lovingly provided for our good, something amazing happens: We find it possible to incorporate healthy boundaries in our own lives.

And it's as we take those steps of spiritual growth that the Almighty wraps His arms around us and begins to open the eyes of our heart. You see, I've come to realize that setting healthy boundaries is first and foremost about love—about the love God has for us, the love He wants us to have for our own lives, and the love He wants us to share with others. Nowhere is God's love through us more needed than with our troubled adult children who can, at times, be incredibly unlovable. Yes, these kids need our love, but they need God's love more.

During His time on earth, Jesus had human limitations, and He accepted them. He needed to sleep and eat; He needed to get away from crowds and be alone with His Father. Jesus also said no to inappropriate behavior, and He spoke the truth in love to those who were stuck or wrong. Jesus offered grace and truth according to people's needs. He modeled what it is to live in God's rhythm of grace, teaching us the importance of boundaries by setting healthy boundaries Himself.

Psychologist and spiritual director Bill Gaultiere put it this way:

> Jesus had personal needs that he put priority on—sometimes even over the needs of other people—and he did so without feeling guilty. Primarily his personal soul care had to do with separating himself from people to be alone with God, who he called "Abba" (Papa). Jesus lived in a rhythm of life that not only kept him free from burnout, but far beyond that it kept him full of God, full of grace and truth, and therefore ready and able to be compassionate and generous in his response to people, their needs, interruptions, and crisis situations.[3]

For many parents of troubled adult children, living in crisis situations has become a way of life, and finding compassion for our kids can sometimes be incredibly hard. Yet God calls us to train up a child in the way he should go, and there really isn't a time frame on that training. God also calls us to love the unlovable, the damaged, and the lost, and our adult children can fall into those categories. So I've learned that it's never too late to parent differently.

Learning to connect with our sons and daughters who lack self-control and are often driven by drugs and damaged thought processes will require our obedience to scriptural truth and, yes, our reliance on God's Spirit to help us.

Obedience

Adhering to boundaries and obeying God's Word don't come naturally. Obedience is something we learn—often through pain. As children grow, they naturally test their boundaries, make mistakes, learn the limits, and eventually grow into full maturity. Unfortunately, this healthy progression may have been subverted by extremely rebellious kids who began taking drugs early in life or who suffered from undiagnosed emotional or mental illnesses. For these troubled children, disobedience became the rule rather than the exception. And sadly, our tendency to react to this disobedience emotionally, rather than to act rationally, often made an incident bigger than it needed to be.

Today, however, many adult children struggle with the very concept of obedience. As they have grown up, we have seen them not only rebel against us, but also against almost every other authority there is— the government, society, law enforcement, employers, and, yes, God. This sinful disobedience can fill a heart with darkness and keep it distant from God and His love.

Can we parents influence the hearts of our adult children, help them push through their pain, and see how much they are loved by God—and by us? Yes. But only in direct proportion to how open and obedient we are to God's divine plan and purpose.

EFFECTIVE STRATEGY

What boundary do you need to set with your troubled adult child? What first step will you take today or tomorrow? And what spiritual growth lessons have you learned lately?

Chapter 5

A Heart Guarded
by God's Love

Margaret is a good wife, mother, and employee. She volunteers in the church nursery every Sunday. She is dependable and conscientious, and she wants to please God as she serves others.

But Margaret has trouble speaking up or asking for help, and lately she's begun to feel exhausted, unsupported, and depressed. At her job, Margaret sits by a rude coworker, the office bully who often has her in tears by the end of the day. Yet, day in and day out, Margaret juggles all her work responsibilities—even some that are technically other people's—and quietly soldiers on. At home, things are even worse. When her 19-year-old son treats her disrespectfully, her husband laughs it off, and neither of them helps around the house. Her heart often aches.

Then, to make matters worse, Margaret discovers her husband is having an affair the same night she realizes her son has stolen her debit card, withdrawn $500 from her checking account, and been arrested for drunk driving. Her already overburdened and unprotected heart is now thoroughly broken.

Clearly, Margaret faces some critical choices. She can continue to make passive and unhealthy choices that leave her heart unprotected, or she can take action and do something entirely different.

And the latter is exactly what Margaret does. Understandably, she is overwhelmed by her emotions and the decisions she needs to make. She doesn't know what her next steps should be. But she is a woman of faith, and God had been preparing her heart for change: He will grow her through pain.

She told me, "My first inclination was to rush to the bank and take out a loan on the house to bail my son out of jail. However, I had recently learned the SANITY steps, and recalling the first step made me literally stop in my tracks, sit down, and reevaluate what to do. When I stopped long enough to be still and pray, I heard the voice of the Spirit loud and clear in my heart. I knew it was time for me to stop my usual responses and to instead TRUST the voice of the Spirit, the *T* step in SANITY."

Knowing she couldn't deal with all these issues and try on new, healthy behaviors on her own, she quickly implemented the *A* step in SANITY: ASSEMBLE supportive people. Within a few hours, a small group of trusted men and women were sitting at her dining room table, praying with her, and confidentially discussing possible steps she could take. Ultimately, the decision would be hers to make, but having input from these wise and godly people helped Margaret apply the *I* step in SANITY and IMPLEMENT a plan of action to get through this time when painful emotions could have crippled her.

And that's how God began healing Margaret's heart.

To find sanity, Margaret also had to accept that she had contributed to her dysfunctional relationship with her son. After years of her coming-to-the-rescue enabling, Margaret had to accept that in many instances she had kept her son from learning the consequences of his actions. She also had to accept that feeling guilty about her past choices wasn't going to help her make better choices now. And she had to take action: She needed, first, to change her perspective on control from seeing control as something that was always bad or wrong to recognizing control as something necessary in the right amount. (Remember, there is a big difference between taking healthy control and being negatively controlling!) By reframing her thoughts, Margaret was able to weather her son's incarceration, the pain of her eventual divorce, and the uncertainty of a life she had never anticipated for herself. In fact, Margaret came through this storm stronger than ever.

Understanding Emotions

When Margaret's world came crashing down, her emotions cut through her heart like a tornado cuts through a town. She felt frightened and betrayed, and she was petrified to be alone. Those emotions were motivating her—as I mentioned— to consider borrowing money to bail her son out of jail. She wanted him to come home, protect her, and make her feel safe. She wanted him to step up to the plate for once and help her.

But taking care of his mother's emotional needs wasn't—and isn't— his responsibility. Furthermore, he was addicted to alcohol and needed professional help, and he was facing serious criminal charges. He was in no condition to meet any of Margaret's needs. Intellectually, she knew that, but her emotions threatened to override her common sense.

In reflecting on her experiences, Margaret realized that she had repeatedly accepted unacceptable behavior from her son and husband by never setting healthy boundaries, by never guarding her heart. Her responses to their negative behavior were equally negative: She would get overly emotional, make excuses for them, blame herself, or adopt a victim mentality. So accustomed to invalidating her emotions and ignoring her heartache, Margaret had disabled her ability to make value-based, God-honoring decisions.

The Heart of the Matter

I, too, ignored my aching heart for years—a fact that made it almost impossible for me to make healthy decisions in any of my relationships. Thankfully, God used Proverbs 4:23 to change my life when my adult son's choices were breaking my heart: "Above all else, guard your heart, for everything you do flows from it." In this Scripture, God is telling us to protect ourselves by—above all else—putting a healthy boundary around our heart. This Scripture set me on course to gain the strength I needed to make tough-love choices in my relationship with my son.

God also used this season to more fully develop my character— to teach me what it meant to mirror the character of Christ and to strengthen my personal relationship with Him, and He continues to use the core message of Proverbs 4:23 to mold me into the person He wants me to be.

Guarding our hearts is not a onetime action. It's an aspect of spiritual growth that—ideally—we come to incorporate throughout our waking hours until it is as natural as breathing. Know, too, that the protective guard we place around our heart is a healthy permanent boundary, not a temporary one.

But notice that God didn't say, "Build an impenetrable ten-foot wall around your heart." God doesn't want us to build a wall that keeps others out, but He knows we need a protective boundary that guards the very place where He lives and the place where we hide His Word.

The New Living Translation of Proverbs 4:23 has powerful implications: "Guard your heart above all else, for it determines the course of your life." Think about it. Something that determines the course of your life should definitely be protected!

Life will never be pain-free, and this call to guard our hearts should not be misconstrued as a way to justify selfishness or to stay safe and isolated from others. We are called to guard and protect our hearts from the deception of the world, the lies of the enemy, and the desires of the flesh. Only then will whatever flows out of our hearts and into the lives of people around us be love.

Created to Love

I am now going to share with you a fundamental truth that needs to be rooted in the deepest part of your heart and mine: We were created for one basic purpose, and that is to love and be loved by God.

When we stop letting ourselves be consumed by the problems of our troubled adult children, we can grow closer to the Lord and develop a life-giving relationship with Him, a relationship that ultimately will change our heart. And with this changed heart we will be better able to love others—especially our struggling children—with His love.

Another reason we struggle to love even our own children with open arms is because we are a target of the enemy, and when he hurts us, it affects the people around us. For example, at the very moment

I'm writing this, I have a good friend texting me about yet another crisis in the life of his adult daughter. He and his wife are consumed with guilt and self-blame, but they aren't to blame for the actions of their daughter. Yet, Satan has convinced them otherwise.

These loving parents have given their child so many chances they've lost count, but her drug addiction and the consequences of her actions have only gotten worse. Sadly, they can't see how their enabling choices have contributed to the drama. They can't see how happy Satan is that he has convinced them it's "all their fault" and thus perpetuates the vicious gerbil wheel of insanity that keeps them and their daughter in bondage.

If only they could see clearly and apply the *S* step and STOP, step back, and allow their daughter to experience the consequences of her actions— perhaps then a true change of heart and character might happen.

This ripple effect of his evil is exactly what the enemy wants. Satan will also assault us by attacking how we think and how we feel. He wants to break our hearts because when he does, he breaks the place where Christ dwells within us. Folks, this is a battle for our hearts and minds. Jesus will never leave us, but when we believe Satan's lies, we push Christ out by accepting responsibility for the actions of our troubled adult children instead of allowing them to experience the spiritual and life growth lesson(s) God wants to teach them.

When Emotions Override Common Sense

Sometimes our emotions can and do get the best of us, especially when they are fueled by the powerful instincts of parental love. Rather than letting emotions control us, let's view those emotions as signals from God. He gets our attention with our emotions, and then He uses them as effective tools that can help us to understand what is going on inside of us. And that understanding—and the help of the Holy Spirit—will help us rein in our emotions when they won't be helpful. To help that understanding, open up your journal and describe a recent incident with your troubled adult child when your emotions fueled your response. What was the root of those emotions? What might have been the outcome of that incident if you had mustered a more impartial attitude? Spend some time on this writing exercise. Ask God to shine a light on the emotions that seem to control you most often. Listen for what He wants to teach you today.

Break the Chain

A host of psychological terms are associated with the reasons why we do the things we do, and one term coined by Sigmund Freud is useful: repetition compulsion. Of course, we human beings are far more complex than any labels and jargon can express, yet in my experience, I have found repetition compulsion to be alive, well, and thriving. In fact, some families have been repeating the same behavior and expecting different results for generations.

If your family is one of those, God can use you to break that chain. He can use you to offer an alternative and build a new bridge of communication. He will begin with a change in your heart—a change that will not go unnoticed by those closest to you.

And that change will be a heart protected—a heart guarded by God's love—that will enable you to see beyond the external symptoms, words, and behaviors that have defined your troubled children in your eyes. So ask God to empower you to respond to your child in a kinder and gentler way.

Remember, you may be the only face of God your son or daughter will see.

EFFECTIVE STRATEGY

Ask the Holy Spirit to help you to first identify and understand your emotions and then to evaluate the emotional health of your heart. To whom are you giving out of authentic love, compassion, honesty, and respect? To whom are you giving from places of guilt, fear, resentment, anger, and bondage to unhealthy repetitive behaviors? Recently, when have your decisions about how you speak and act in a given situation helped the people you love? When have your decisions hurt them in some way? Also, in your notebook, list what God is calling you to do to guard your heart.

Chapter 6

Inside and Outside: What's Really Going On?

I have a plaque hanging by my front door that constantly reminds me how I need to view not only those closest to me, but also, when possible, the world in which I live. It reads, *Open the eyes of my heart, Lord.*

If our hearts aren't open, we probably won't see the internal illnesses that have transformed our adult children into people we barely recognize. So often, the external words and actions—that are impossible *not* to see—blind us to what's really going on. Clearly, Satan has devised a brilliant strategy for not only keeping our kids in bondage but also keeping us parents from identifying the real issue at hand.

I recently received the following cry for help from a reader who could not see past the externals. He was completely unable to see what was really going on in the heart of his son:

> *My wife and I have been caught up in the chaotic mess of our son's life for so long that nothing makes sense anymore. He looks pretty much like a bum most of the time. He refuses to keep himself or his room clean, and it keeps getting worse. He leaves dirty dishes everywhere, lights on in every room he goes through, and if we have guests, we are embarrassed to let them use our guest bath, which is his bathroom, because it's disgusting! He*

won't help with anything unless he is asked repeatedly. Zero initiative. He almost never goes outside. And he's gained so much weight that he doesn't even look like himself.

Both my wife and I work, and it would be nice if he helped out, but asking him to do anything ends up in a battle, so we've stopped asking. We never know when to speak up or when to stay quiet—and this walking on eggshells is exhausting. We just can't understand how someone can be so lazy. After he lost his job, he moved back home for a few months to get things together—and it's now been three years. Three very long years!

Things need to change—and soon! But we don't even know where to start. We're ready to put everything he owns in cardboard boxes and move him to one of those weekly rental motels, but without someone taking care of him, we don't think he'll last very long. What should we do?

Many factors are contributing to the chaotic mess described here. Addressing all that is going on will take a good amount of effort, time, and prayer. But the fact that a few months turned into three years clearly indicates that the situation is about more than their son's apparent "laziness." These parents would do well to consider how they've been responding to their son and that laziness for these three very long years.

Before these parents—who are understandably frustrated and angry—said or did anything rash, I urged them to first apply the *S* step in SANITY and STOP. They needed to step back and identify all the external issues driving them crazy. "Sit down with your wife and make a list of every external issue you see that is bothering you. Do this rationally and not emotionally," I wrote back. "Then let's talk about how or if these external issues may be covering up something more."

Seeing Through the Fog

When have you searched high and low for something only to find it right in front of your face? When that happens to me (and it does more often than I care to admit), I can sometimes hear my mom's voice in my head, speaking to me as a little girl: "Allison, it's right in front of your nose. If it were a dog, it would have bitten you!"

Sometimes, though, we need help when we aren't seeing the things we need to see. What better help than this verse from Psalm 119: "Your word is a lamp for my feet, a light on my path" (verse 105).

When we want to connect to our troubled adult children in a way that can make a difference, we are wise to first separate our children's external issues from their internal illnesses. If we truly want to connect with our adult children and find sanity, we have to start seeing things differently. We must reframe our thinking and change our perspective so that we can see what lies beneath the aggravating and exhausting surface.

Also, if we're not careful, all of our child's external issues that trigger us will come to the surface, and embarrassment, anger, and just plain frustration will fuel a lashing out we will later regret.

Taking Healthy Control

Being able to determine whether we're dealing with lazy, selfish, or manipulative adult children who are fully capable of carrying their weight and just need to pack up and go or genuinely troubled children who are battling emotional and mental illnesses is a huge responsibility for us parents. Children in this second category aren't necessarily lazy or rebellious. They simply don't have the emotional or mental ability to function well. Mental illness often lurks behind a seemingly healthy face and voice. But the chemical imbalances in the body do strange things to the brain. These invisible issues and internal illnesses are often factors in our troubled adult child's inability to hold a job, think rationally, exercise self-control, resist drugs, and sometimes simply take a shower.

Additionally, when changes must be made, it's important we choose a godly way to approach a situation—a way to take control that can actually bring about change. For instance, if we're not very careful, when our adult children are struggling with emotional and mental illness or substance abuse disorders, we may find ourselves treating them like little kids, reminding them to take a shower, brush their teeth, change their clothes, and pick up after themselves. This condescending treatment does little to instill positive self-confidence in children who may be teetering precariously on the edge of depression or feeling suicidal.

Parents who need to make this determination between attitudinal and physiological roots of their adult children's actions can turn to God for the wisdom and spiritual discernment this challenge demands. The following examples of both the external and the internal aspects of a child's behavior may also help you determine what yours is dealing with:

Scenario 1

External: Your son rarely brushes his teeth. His hair is greasy, and when he leaves his room (which isn't often), he walks around in a stinky bathrobe. He's gained a significant amount of weight, and he leaves dirty dishes all over the house. He never makes his bed, and he refuses to clean anything in the house, even his own room. The only thing he seems at all interested in is playing video games—which he does almost all day long. "I'm going to throw that thing away!" you say. Clearly, the Xbox is the culprit.

When you consider these externals, your son seems to be lazy and taking advantage of your support. You didn't train him to be this way. You blame his laziness on the lifestyle and the friends he had before, or the broken heart he experienced when his fiancée gave the ring back, or the fact that he just lost another job. The kid just can't seem to get a break. But these external issues are not getting better, and you're ready to explode.

Internal: The lack of hope in your son's eyes, his lack of motivation, and his apparent laziness could be indicative of serious clinical depression that can sometimes be a catalyst to hopeless and suicidal thoughts. PTSD and anxiety disorders may also be contributing factors.

Clinical depression calls for professional help, and it's critical that our troubled kids seek a diagnosis from a doctor if we have seen these symptoms. Although we cannot force our children to seek that help, we'll look at some effective strategies we can implement to encourage and/or intervene on their behalf to assist them in getting professional help, even if they are in denial of the need—which many of them are.

Scenario 2

External: Your adult child is constantly battling financial problems. She routinely cannot pay her bills, and her utilities are frequently disconnected. She gambles regularly. Scratch tickets are her ever-present companion, even though she can't pay her rent. She doesn't seem to have trouble getting a job, but she can't seem to keep one. When she gets moody and nasty—and it happens often—she snaps at anyone who looks at her sideways.

Internal: The inability to keep a job and meet responsibilities (such as paying bills) could be the result of bipolar disorder, depression, or substance abuse. Your daughter may also be self-medicating to try to control the highs and lows caused by her disorder.

Scenario 3

External: Your son comes home drunk, high, or both. He gets arrested and loses his job, which for the first time in a long time was a job he actually enjoyed.

Internal: Substance abuse disorders are often as complex as mental illness. Your son is self-medicating for a reason. Do you know what it is? Knowing that there is a root, a culprit behind his actions, is helpful; finding out what that root is can be difficult. One helpful skill is being able to ask the right questions in the right way as you provide your children with the safety they need to be candid and vulnerable. But the reality is, you are not his therapist, you are not her counselor, and the emotional stability of an addict is precarious. Any concerns you voice would most likely prompt an angry and defensive response. Additionally, many addicts fight mental illness as well, and taking drugs is their way of coping. Yes, that combination of addiction and mental illness greatly complicates their lives.

What We Can't See

We can't see what is happening in our lungs when we have pneumonia, but difficulty in breathing and a cough are external symptoms that can tip us off that something is going on. Similarly, when we have the stomach flu, we can't see the bacteria raging through our intestines, but we can definitely identify the symptoms. Like these diseases, the cause of mental illness is not visible to the naked eye. And that's what makes identifying this problem and finding the right help so difficult.

Key to identifying the issue is separating the external from the internal. And, yes, that can be problematic, if not completely beyond a parent's ability. Being able to see what is happening on the outside is relatively easy, but the same cannot be said for what is happening on the inside. That's why getting a professional opinion and diagnosis is critical.

While it's true that we can't force our adult kids to get to the root of their problems, we *can* learn effective ways to approach them and to show our desire to connect with them, not control them. And may God use that desire to open their eyes to a new hope for healing.

As we step back and separate the external issues from the internal illnesses, we can begin to ask the hard questions:

1. How emotionally, psychologically, and mentally damaged is my child?

2. What degree of independence is realistically possible?

3. How much long-term support and care will I actually be able and/or wise to give?

4. What does *my child* (not his mom or dad) want to do with his life? Purpose changes things. Purpose gives us a reason to live. To get out of bed. To take a shower.

5. Has your child lost hope? If so, pray for wisdom to know what you can do to help her find it.

God is our hope for our troubled adult children. We must rest in His power, His kindness, His faithfulness, and His goodness. And whenever possible, we must introduce our children to the hope we have in Him—and may we do so in ways that will begin to soften their hearts.

What is one way to share our hope with our children? Well, call me old school, but I'm a diehard believer in the powerful role a refrigerator door has in the family. Acting as a bulletin board, that door is prime real estate for posting encouraging words and Scripture—and it's guaranteed to be seen by your offspring several times throughout the day if they're living at home. Jeremiah 29:11 is a good verse to keep visible: "'I know the plans I have for you,' declares the LORD, 'plans to prosper you and not to harm you, plans to give you hope and a future.'"

Sadly, many of our sons and daughters have forgotten what hope is.

God's Love Is Hope

I love David's words at the end of Psalm 23: "Goodness and love will follow me all the days of my life" (verse 6). The Hebrew word translated as *follow* means "to chase, to pursue." David proclaimed that God's goodness and love chased him. I love that.

And God's goodness and love do not chase only David. Goodness and love are part of our Creator's DNA, of His very being. So we can be absolutely positive that God's goodness and love are chasing our kids too. Pray the *S* step in SANITY for them. Pray that they will STOP and let Him catch them!

Maybe we need to slow down and let God catch us too. We've been chasing our kids for so long, we've forgotten that we also need God's goodness and love. Sometimes we focus so much on our pain and the external problems that we forget to look inside our own hearts. When we do so, however, we'll be reminded that we need hope and healing at least as much as our children do. Also like our children, we need to fall into our Father God's arms.

So are you ready to do the hard work of separating the external issues from the internal illnesses, of focusing on the truth, and of reframing your strategies according to the illness your child battles? Frankly, I'm not sure any one of us parents is ever ready, but in our very weakness, we can experience God's great strength (2 Corinthians 12:10). Go in God's grace as you do this hard but invaluable work of determining what external and internal issues are impacting your child.

EFFECTIVE STRATEGY

Take time to write down everything you see in your child's appearance, behaviors, attitudes, and decisions. Then start researching what these external symptoms may be pointing to and/or hiding. There are several excellent websites that can shed some much-needed light on the problems many of our children struggle with, starting with NAMI.org, the National Alliance on Mental Illness. But remember, the goal isn't to be an armchair doctor and diagnose your kids after reading a couple articles on the web. Obtaining a professional diagnosis and prognosis at some point may be critical to your child's current situation and future possibilities.

One more thing. Know that the process of research and education can help to open our eyes to other possibilities for connecting with our children, such as learning better ways to communicate or how to instill confidence through developing enhanced coping mechanisms. Furthermore, our perspective on the present and the future can also change when we start to see our children as people who need to be loved, not problems that need to be solved.

Chapter 7

Befuddled Brains: Substance Abuse and Mental Illness

Many of our struggling kids have a disease—a brain disorder that affects most if not all areas of life. Parents might call it addiction; professionals call it a substance abuse disorder.

The principal feature of a substance abuse disorder is a cluster of cognitive, behavioral, and psychological symptoms indicative of continued use. In other words, the way our troubled adult children perceive or process knowledge (cognition), the way they respond to and react to what is going on around them (behavior), and their functions of awareness, feeling, and motivation (psychology) have all been diminished by the drugs that have damaged their brain.

These children often make terrible decisions with tragic or destructive consequences and may endanger themselves, their loved ones, and their livelihood. They are more likely to miss school or work, get in trouble with the law, and have increased health problems. Substance abusers, due to their chemical dependency, are usually unable to change their habits on their own without focused professional or medical help. Many parents have been running themselves ragged trying to second-guess and rescue these troubled kids.

A National Epidemic

While alcohol abuse is still a significant problem in our society, the substance abuse creating the most havoc today is drugs, particularly opioids. Generally known as a class of painkillers, opioids range from illegal heroin to legally available pain medications.

Opioid pain relievers are generally safe when taken for a short time and as prescribed by a doctor, but because they produce euphoria in addition to pain relief, they can be misused (taken in a different way or in a larger quantity than prescribed or without a doctor's prescription). Regular use—even as prescribed by a doctor—can lead to dependence and, when misused, opioid pain relievers can cause serious health problems, become dangerously addictive, and lead to overdose incidents and death.

A Painful Truth

When it comes to the behavior of addicts, we must confront a painful truth. One resource puts it this way:

> The addicted person will use defense mechanisms such as denial, blaming, rationalization and manipulation to get what they need. They start seeing the world, not as it is, but as they need it to be to sustain their addiction. They will lie, bargain, deny and steal from you when you're not looking. They will make promises they are incapable of keeping. "I'll pay you back soon." "I'll stop soon."

> They will blame you (or anyone else who is handy) for their addiction, job losses, and unattended responsibilities. Their habit becomes their whole world, and thus completely occupies all their thoughts. When can they use again? How do they get the money to pay for it? Where can they crash while they're high?

> What is difficult for many parents to understand is how the brain is completely overrun by the addiction. Your child has not become an evil person—their addiction has clouded their judgment and made them essentially incapable of operating like they would if they were sober. They are still inside but are no longer in the driver's seat.[1]

As parents, we know this on some level, but our initial response is to try and help them out of love. We pay their bills, cater to their needs, and make excuses for them. While these things seem like compassion, they are perpetuating the disease and further endangering our children.

Befuddled Brains

It's hard to admit that many of the drugs our children have depended on have left severe scars—some irreparable. And watching them suffer consequences that alter their lives in irreversible ways is more than heartbreaking—it's devastating.

There is a persistent underlying change in brain chemistry lasting beyond detoxification. In plain language, this means that even if someone stops using drugs, in most cases the damage has already been done.

The brain is the most complex organ in the body, and brain damage can result in deficits and impairments that make everyday life activities and social functioning more difficult. And some damage leaves people severely impaired and unable to function without a closely monitored structure for the remainder of their life.

Knowledge Is Power

After years of caustic choices, massive mistakes, and a long list of catastrophic consequences, many of our kids have reached the end of their ropes with nowhere to go. They're bouncing around like balls in a pinball machine. More than a few have virtually no frame of reference for right and wrong, some have a distorted or narcissistic view of their importance in the lives of everyone they know, and for many, their threshold for withstanding pain—in any amount—is almost zero.

And so, they do whatever possible to numb it.

While the statistics are frightening, the firsthand experiences of parents who contact me are nothing short of horrific. I hear endless stories of heartbreak, of repeated cycles of rehab and relapse, of children broken by their addictions and families destroyed by the consequences. While we can't single-handedly fix the widespread epidemic, we can become informed as parents, thus enabling us to make choices that can hopefully help our children who are in serious trouble.

If our goal is to connect to our troubled adult children in ways that can help and not handicap, we must proactively learn not only about the substances that have taken control of our children but also about the related mental and emotional issues that we seldom understand. We cannot bury our heads in the sand and shut the door on the problem because it will keep knocking down the doors. Remember, we cannot (and should not) try to be their therapists or counselors, but with increased knowledge, we can arm ourselves for this battle.

Dual Diagnosis

Also referred to as *co-occurring disorders*, dual diagnosis is a term for when someone experiences a substance abuse disorder and a mental illness simultaneously. Much like the age-old question of, "Which came first, the chicken or the egg?" it's hard to pinpoint whether a mental illness led to a substance abuse problem or vice versa. People experiencing a mental health condition may turn to alcohol or other drugs as a form of self-medication to improve the mental health symptoms they experience. However, research shows that alcohol and other drugs worsen the symptoms of mental illnesses.

Many of our troubled kids are dealing with a dual diagnosis. If you're a parent who is considering advocating on behalf of your adult child, it is critical that you understand something problematic about this diagnosis. The professional fields of mental health and substance abuse recovery have *entirely different cultures*, so finding integrated care can be challenging. When seeking counselors or programs, ask questions about whether they are equipped to help someone with *both diagnoses*, if that is required.

Identifying the Signs of Mental Illness

I used to think the poor choices my adult child consistently made were due to his willful defiance and impulsive actions— that he knew better but just chose not to do the right thing. Now, after so many years, I'm beginning to think there might be something seriously wrong with his thinking—with his mind. It's not like he's crazy or anything like that, but something isn't right. How can I tell if my troubled adult child is mentally ill?

It is difficult to imagine, but 50 percent of adults will experience mental illness in their lifetime.[2] There's no simple test to distinguish between mental illness and typical behaviors. Trying to tell the difference between what expected behaviors are and what might be the signs of a mental illness isn't always easy.

Each illness has its own symptoms, but common signs of mental illness in adults and adolescents can include the following:

- Excessive worrying or fear
- Feeling excessively sad or low
- Confused thinking or problems concentrating and learning
- Extreme mood changes, including uncontrollable "highs" or feelings of euphoria
- Prolonged or strong feelings of irritability or anger
- Avoiding friends and social activities
- Difficulties understanding or relating to other people
- Changes in sleeping habits or feeling tired and low energy
- Changes in eating habits, such as increased hunger or lack of appetite
- Difficulty perceiving reality (delusions or hallucinations, in which a person experiences and senses things that don't exist in objective reality)
- Inability to perceive changes in one's own feelings, behavior, or personality
- Abuse of substances like alcohol or drugs (thus a dual diagnosis)
- Multiple physical ailments without obvious causes (such as headaches, stomach aches, vague and ongoing "aches and pains")

- Thinking about suicide
- Inability to carry out daily activities or handle everyday problems and stress.[3]

I get it that we don't want to think about these things. But you're reading this book—so you're apparently thinking about these things. Let's roll out the *S* step once again and STOP. Stop pretending you don't know there's a serious problem, and start learning everything you can about how to effect positive change.

Let's start with educating ourselves about one of the most prevalent forms of mental illness today—depression.

Depression

We all feel sad from time to time—it's part of being human. However, being sad is not the same as suffering from true clinical depression, which is something else entirely. The symptoms are different for everyone who suffers with it and can often linger for weeks, months, and perhaps years. Major depression is one of the most common mental disorders in the United States. For some individuals, it can result in severe impairments that interfere with or limit one's ability to carry out significant life activities.

Depression (major depressive disorder or clinical depression) is a common but severe mood disorder. It causes severe symptoms that affect how you feel, think, and handle daily activities such as sleeping, eating, or working. To be diagnosed with depression, the symptoms must be present for at least two weeks.

If your son or daughter lives with you, it may be easier for you to identify if they have been experiencing some of the following signs and symptoms. This is what to look for that indicates they may be suffering from depression:

- Persistent sad, anxious, or "empty" mood
- Feelings of hopelessness or pessimism
- Irritability
- Feelings of guilt, worthlessness, or helplessness

- Loss of interest or pleasure in hobbies and activities
- Decreased energy or fatigue
- Moving or talking more slowly
- Feeling restless or having trouble sitting still
- Difficulty concentrating, remembering, or making decisions
- Difficulty sleeping, early-morning awakening, or oversleeping
- Appetite and/or weight changes
- Thoughts of death or suicide, or suicide attempts
- Aches or pains, headaches, cramps, or digestive problems without an apparent physical cause and/or that do not ease even with treatment

Not everyone who is depressed experiences every symptom. Some people experience only a few signs, while others may experience many. In all cases, symptoms of depression, however few or many, should not be ignored. The sense of hopelessness that depression often carries can be life threatening. Some forms of depression are slightly different, or they may develop under unique circumstances, such as:

- Persistent depressive disorder
- Postpartum depression
- Psychotic depression
- Seasonal affective disorder
- Bipolar disorder—different from depression, but it is included in this list because someone with bipolar disorder experiences episodes of extremely low moods that meet the criteria for major depression (called "bipolar depression")

Bipolar and Related Disorders

Another predominant illness our offspring struggle with is bipolar disorder, also known as manic-depressive illness. This brain disorder causes unusual shifts in mood, energy, activity levels, and the ability to carry out day-to-day tasks.

People with bipolar disorder experience periods of unusually intense emotion, changes in sleep patterns and activity levels, and unusual behaviors. These distinct periods are called "mood episodes." Mood episodes are drastically different from the moods and behaviors that are typical for the person. Extreme changes in energy, activity, and sleep go along with mood episodes.

There are four basic types of bipolar disorder; all of them involve visible changes in mood, energy, and activity levels. These moods range from periods of extremely "up," elated, and energized behavior (known as manic episodes) to very sad, "down," or hopeless periods (known as depressive episodes). Visit the NAMI.org website to learn more about:

- Bipolar I Disorder
- Bipolar II Disorder
- Cyclothymic Disorder
- Other Specified and Unspecified Bipolar and Related Disorders

Prepare for Battle

If we have a child who is addicted to drugs or alcohol or exhibits signs of emotional or mental illness, we can no longer just pass it off as "He just had a little too much to drink," or "She just needed some help to stay awake studying and to take the edge off the stress of school," or "He's always marched to a different drummer; it's part of his unique character." Instead, we must equip ourselves with the reality of what our culture is facing in the form of substance abuse and mental illness—and what we can do to encourage our kids to get the help they desperately need.

Sadly, many of our kids are deep in denial and unwilling to get help. However, that doesn't mean we can't seek help for ourselves and our family. Find out now what resources are available to you. Conduct an online search, ask your pastor, or reach out to another parent who you know is struggling with this issue. Apply the *A* step in SANITY and

ASSEMBLE supportive people around you that can help you discern the best ways to help yourself and your troubled adult child without enabling or excuses.

Remember, unless we have been declared their legal guardian (something we will talk about in a later chapter), we cannot force an adult child to go into rehab, or to seek a professional counselor, and/ or to attend AA or NA meetings, no matter how much they need to. However, if you have agreed to allow your adult child to live with you, you have every right to make seeking help a mandatory requirement in exchange for the roof over their head that you are willing to provide. It is their choice to refuse, in which case the offer to reside in your home, no matter how short term—should also be refused.

This is tough love.

This is accountability.

This is consequences in action.

Suicide

Depression and suicide are on the rise in our country. The American Foundation for Suicide Prevention reports that the suicide rate is higher than ever and kills more of us than car accidents do. It is "responsible for 44,965 deaths per year; that's an average of 123 per day."[4]

Staggering, isn't it?

While there is no single reason for suicide, mental illness plays a significant factor, particularly when a depressive disorder or bipolar disorder is a component. Severe stress and insufficient coping skills are also factors. With statistics like these, it's crucial that we acknowledge the suicidal feelings our troubled adult children struggle with and encourage them to seek professional help. And once again, it is vital that we speak hope into their lives.

When you suspect someone is in trouble, you can offer them support and assistance getting help. If you're concerned, you should ask directly if they are having thoughts about suicide. Open up the subject, look them in the eye, and show them you care and want to be there for them. Be calm on the outside—even if you're hysterical on the inside.

Depression and suicide can be tricky to talk about. The more we know about these, the more prepared we will be if and when we need to address them. Keeping open the lines of communication is vital. Education is essential in preventing suicide. Each of us can play a significant role in helping those around us who struggle with these emotions on this journey to survival.

If you or someone you know may be suicidal, call the National Suicide Prevention Lifeline *now* at 1-800-273-8255. Don't wait until it's too late.

Moving Forward

In the next chapter, we're going to talk about the need for our troubled children to get a professional diagnosis and prognosis. As we begin that journey, there are still things we can do right now to help them.

First, we can get help ourselves.

We can pray for the courage and wisdom to change the things we can—starting with ourselves.

If we are struggling with depression or other mental illness and do not get help coping with it and treating it, how can we expect our troubled adult children to desire that kind of help for themselves? The positive changes they see in us can influence our kids to do the same. The improvements we make in attitude, energy, and even countenance through getting help ourselves can motivate and inspire others. Especially when they see that the key source of our dependence is the truth found in Scripture.

Secondly, we can get smart. We can educate ourselves about substance abuse and mental illness, and the signs and symptoms. We can read Christian books concerning depression, bipolar, addiction, and search the web for articles about how we can help. We can pray with and talk to our faith counselors and friends as we apply the *A* step in SANITY and ASSEMBLE a support group to talk to and share our experiences with. We can encourage our children to join a support group as well. We can learn effective strategies that include developing written plans as we apply the *I* step in SANITY and IMPLEMENT a plan of action that identifies explicitly the support we are able to provide to address the emotional and mental health needs of our child.

And we can read and share Scripture that protects our hearts and minds as we apply the *Y* step in SANITY and YIELD everything to the God of all creation, Who knows the plans He has for us—and our troubled adult children.

Instill Hope

Many of our struggling sons and daughters have lost hope. Unable to see beyond the fog of depression, mental illness, or addiction, they are lost. And it's our job to assure them they are not—that God is standing by, ever ready to pour His help, healing, and hope into their troubled lives. Christian hope is an optimistic assurance from God that something will be fulfilled.[5] As believers, we can count on God's guaranteed promises of hope.

Parents, we must speak words of Christian hope and love into the hearts and minds of our troubled children. Beware not to preach. Don't force your faith on them—merely let the character of Christ flow from your heart into theirs. Let God do the work. God has His hand on them, even if they don't see or feel it.

In addition to taking proactive measures that address substance abuse and mental illness, encourage them to seek solace in God's Word, and provide them with a Bible if they don't have one. Whatever our problems or needs, the answers can be found in His Word.

EFFECTIVE STRATEGY

Search your own heart and ask God to reveal ways you can show His love to your addicted and/or mentally ill son or daughter. Let your troubled adult child see God at work. Specifically, ask God to show you how to speak hope into their life and what actions you should take.

Chapter 8

Diagnosis and Prognosis

M any of our kids need extensive evaluation, counseling, medications, and a treatment team all working together to help them walk toward healing and hope.

Having your child get the proper diagnosis from a professional Mental Health Provider (MHP) is key to knowing how to move forward. If there hasn't been an actual medical and psychological diagnosis, it can be difficult for your child to get the treatment they need.

The words *diagnosis* and *prognosis* are commonly (though not exclusively) used in the field of medicine. Both terms contain the root word *gnosis*, which means "knowledge." But *diagnosis* and *prognosis* refer to different kinds of knowledge or information.

In the medical field, *diagnosis* relates to identifying and understanding the nature of a disease or disorder, while a *prognosis* is a prediction of the probable outcome of a disease or disorder. In essence, what we're looking at is "what is" (diagnosis)…and "what's possible" (prognosis).

Until we can truthfully discover "what is," our ability to identify "what's possible" is an impossibility.

Remove the Blinders

The route by which many of our kids have arrived at making their choices has been filled with situations and circumstances most of us would find hard to comprehend, much less experience firsthand as they have. These life experiences—many traumatic—have significantly impacted their lives, often leaving emotional scars.

Without a doubt, the "bad stuff" of life has affected our children. Sadly, long-term substance abuse, untreated mental illness, traumatic life experiences, painful memories, and unhealthy lifestyle choices have taken their toll on our kids. These aren't just kids who push us to the end of our rope or frustrate us to no end.

Our troubled adult children are battered, bruised, and broken. Getting a professional diagnosis means dredging up years of memories—not all of which are pleasant. As desperate as you are to understand what your child is dealing with, you must apply the *S* step and STOP, step back, and proceed with care and caution.

I'm not sure I entirely realized how traumatic the process would be until the day my son completed a lengthy mental health assessment test. He was applying for Social Security disability, and the process was grueling.

I drove him to the appointment and brought work to do while I waited in the car. After two hours, Chris walked out of the building, and I could tell by his body language that something wasn't right. He slid into the front seat, and I could almost feel the weight of the pain that he carried with him.

"What's the matter? What happened?" I asked.

I watched as he slowly shook his head, bit his trembling lip, and fought back the tears that began to drip down his cheeks slowly.

Chris is not a crier. He's spent a great many years developing the tough-guy persona that kept him safe on the streets and in prison. But that day was different.

"Man, I'm so messed up, Mom," he said slowly and quietly while shaking his head. "The things they asked me…man, oh man…" He couldn't articulate what he wanted to say, but I could sense at that moment my son felt fundamentally broken.

Parents, it's crucial that we remain sensitive to what is happening in the hearts and minds of our sons or daughters as they are poked, prodded, assessed, and made to recall things they would rather forget. It's like being on an emotional roller coaster with one appointment after another over a period of weeks—sometimes even months.

I wasn't prepared to see, much less respond to, the raw pain on my son's face that day. My heart broke in a way I had never before felt. His countenance, posture, and noticeable pain branded my heart.

If you're walking closely with your struggling child on their diagnosis journey, be prepared to look beyond what you initially see. Realize that their refusal to obtain a diagnosis may be fear. Ask the Lord to open the eyes of your heart and to give you the words and actions of hope and comfort that your child needs the most.

A Journey of Discovery

Diagnosing mental illness as well as the damage of substance abuse is critical. A diagnosis can lead to treatment, functionality, and, hopefully, a better quality of life for everyone. There is no shame in seeking help.

I've received thousands of emails from parents whose troubled adult children refuse to acknowledge their substance abuse or mental illnesses. How my heart aches for the countless desperate parents who are struggling to do the right thing—yet, uncertain what that is.

Sadly, no matter how much we want to help kids who desperately need help, the fact is, in many instances, our hands are tied. Our struggling children are adults, and as such, we cannot force them to get a diagnosis. We cannot insist they seek treatment or take medication if they don't want it.

Forcing adult children to do anything only causes a chasm of mistrust and a feeling of isolation and also causes them to be resistant. Their willing cooperation is key to proper and adequate diagnosis and treatment.

So, in mapping out your strategy, make critical decisions by prayer and careful, rational thought, not emotion.

In the event your child refuses to seek help or denies that help is even needed, you are faced with a challenging but not impossible hurdle to jump. How serious are you about helping your child? Do you really think they have emotional, mental, and perhaps even substance abuse issues that have altered their life and could possibly end their life if not addressed? If so, the time for pretense is over. It's time for an intervention. And one of the first ways to intervene is to stop making life comfortable for them. To stop giving with no expectation of receiving.

We've been talking a lot about the "living situation issue," a critical component in many family dynamics today. Often a challenging situation for everyone, this is an instance where having your son or daughter under your roof can bring them closer to getting the professional help they need. But only if you're willing to take healthy control, follow up on the consequences you establish, and say what you mean and mean what you say.

Parents, if your troubled adult child lives with you or will be coming home to live shortly, you are in a dominant position. You can make getting a mental health diagnosis a mandatory requirement for them to be given the opportunity to live in your home. Think of this like providing proof of automobile insurance to register your vehicle. You must do one before acquiring the other.

Let's face it, we aren't dealing with typical, run-of-the-mill situations or circumstances. We're looking at the emotional, mental, and physical health of our sons and daughters. In many cases, we're looking at the difference between them having a future or saying goodbye to one. And so, this mandatory requirement of obtaining a professional diagnosis needs to be listed in your Residential Agreement, along with the consequences you have established if they do not comply.

Your declaration of what is needed for them to live in your home is entirely acceptable. You are not forcing them to get a diagnosis. It is their choice.

This may sound cold and calculated, but this is an instance where you need to reframe your thinking. We're talking about boundaries, responsibility, accountability, and consequences from choices. It's time for them to give—or you will take.

No diagnosis, no shelter. The choice will be up to them.

Following up on the consequences will be up to you.

However, if we genuinely feel their life depends on it and they are incapable of making a rational decision, the only way we can override their choice is to take legal steps that give us the power to make choices for them. I talk about the "guardianship" process in chapter 14, "Healthy Support and Compassionate Communication," and it's one that should not be entered into lightly.

So then, what do we do? Let the chips fall where they may? Or do everything in our power to support and encourage them to get the help we think they need?

My vote is on the latter.

Is It Really Denial?

Until I began to educate myself on the diagnostic classifications of substance abuse disorders and mental illness, I used to think denial was the choice of an obstinate, manipulative, and self-serving individual. Imagine my surprise when I learned our kids' denial has a name.

It's actually a condition, a state of mind. The brain does weird things, and this is one of them. The name for this denial of diagnosis is Anosognosia (ano-sog-no-sia).

Damage to the frontal lobe in a person's brain can cause this condition. Mental illnesses such as schizophrenia and bipolar disorder, the use of drugs, or some diseases can cause damage to the frontal lobe. This damage affects the person's ability to take in the diagnosis and update their self-image. In other words, they still see themselves as they were before the illness. (Not unlike some of us parents.)

> Anosognosia affects 50% of people with schizophrenia and 40% of people with bipolar disorder. It can also accompany illnesses such as major depression with psychotic features. Treating these mental health conditions is much more complicated if lack of insight is one of the symptoms. People with Anosognosia are placed at increased risk of homelessness or arrest. Learning to understand Anosognosia and its risks can improve the odds of helping people with this difficult symptom.[1]

If your son or daughter refuses to acknowledge their diagnosis, it could be they are suffering from this condition. They are not trying to be difficult or delusional; *they just cannot grasp the concept of their deficit.* If denial plays a part in your relationship dynamic, it's critical to pray for wisdom and discernment concerning what to do next. You must act from a place of rational thinking and not emotional feeling. Is your troubled adult child suffering from Anosognosia, or is something else going on? Talk to a professional.

Their Willingness

The conditions our troubled adult children experience are often difficult to diagnose. Unlike a broken arm, a bacterial infection, or the flu or pneumonia, there are many hidden variables with a mental health condition—even more so if a dual diagnosis substance abuse disorder is a component.

Determining their need and capability will require assessment—and this isn't something that happens in a 20-minute doctor appointment. What we are talking about involves answering endless questions, filling out countless forms, taking tests, undergoing physical and psychological examinations, and participating in evaluations that in the end will determine the level of ability and/or incapacitation your adult child truly has.

Learning to navigate the mental health system can be a daunting task for a reasonably healthy individual. For some of our kids, it will seem like climbing Mount Everest. It will take perseverance and patience to overcome obstacles and make it through the paperwork process. Should your child elect to soldier on and do it alone, your support and prayers will be needed more than ever. However, if your struggling son or daughter allows you to help during this process, it will be an excellent opportunity to introduce them to what team building looks like.

This isn't about you taking charge and handling everything; it's about you and your son or daughter working together as a team to achieve a common goal.

Financial Frustration

Not all troubled adult children are in denial or just unwilling to get help. In many cases, their hesitancy in seeing a doctor is financial. If they agree to see someone for a diagnosis, who will pay for it? There's a good chance your child does not have insurance or the funds, and they are most likely no longer on your health insurance plan.

That said, are you willing to pay for the doctor's visit and testing? Taking these tests and having results analyzed can be costly. If you do not have the funds, are you ready to navigate the process with your child to file for government assistance?

When my son lived with me several years ago during his 18-month probation, he began the process of applying for Social Security disability. At the same time, he needed to apply for emergency medical care and food stamps.

I'm an organized person, but I had no idea just how challenging this can be. Filling out this form, filing that paperwork, making sure a copy of this form gets to that person, and so on. Staying on top of everything is almost like a part-time job. For parents who want—need—to help in any way possible, there's something you can do right now that might seem insignificant—but that is anything but.

How to Be Helpful Right Now

Whether private or state run, mental health and substance abuse health providers and centers will provide your child with a lot of information at intake. In the case of a state agency, you can depend on that paperwork to be extensive.

This is a great deal of information to process, not to mention to keep organized. Remember, none of this is about what *you* need or want. It's information *your child* needs to help them feel whole. Encourage them to read everything they receive and file it for future reference. Teach them to start to take charge of their life.

As your child begins the process of getting a professional diagnosis and prognosis, there is something you can provide that will be of immeasurable worth as time passes: a file system.

Don't laugh. Chances are, your offspring has little in the way of a system to maintain and track what is going to become a plethora of paperwork very quickly.

Go to a local office supply store and buy one of those small, portable file boxes with a handle. The kind that will hold hanging folders. Buy a package of those hanging folders, as well as a package of file folders. Now, using the clear plastic tabs that come with the hanging folders, make the sections listed below, and place empty files in each section. Trust me; these file folders won't be empty for long.

- Financial
- Health History
- Information & Research
- Insurance
- Legal
- Medications
- SSI/Disability
- Treatment Team
- Misc.

Navigating the System

Most of us are already familiar with how emergency rooms, hospitalization, and private practice works. But what to expect when mental health centers and institutions or substance abuse centers come into play leaves many of us clueless. Every state has different laws and policies, so it's important that your adult child becomes familiar with those that apply to them in their state.

The first step we often take when faced with health issues is a visit to our Primary Care Provider (PCP). In many circumstances, the relationship some patients have with their PCP is often a close one, so it's typically more comfortable to share their concerns with them before seeking a psychologist or psychiatrist. Although they are not trained as mental health specialists, they generally are on the front lines and can initially diagnose and start a treatment process by managing the presented condition through prescriptions.

However, some of our children don't have a connection with a "first responder" PCP. In which case, they may be starting from scratch. Help them ask for provider referrals and conduct online research. Parents, it's vital that you encourage them not to call the first name they see online. Some mental health care providers specialize in treating PTSD patients, or domestic violence survivors, or self-harm cutters. If they welcome your involvement, help your son or daughter do their homework.

"Get all the advice and instruction you can, so you will be wise," instructs Proverbs 19:20 (NLT).

This is the time that if you have medical records from your child's past, you obtain copies and provide them to your child—for storage in their file box.

A Process of Discovery

Before you begin this journey with your adult child, it's important to note that it really will be a *journey*. This isn't a quick or natural process. It may take time to find the right doctors, counselors, medications, and therapeutic methods to address your child's specific issues.

Parents, you can choose to keep the status quo and let things go on as they have, or perhaps even grow worse. Or, you can implement a new plan of action that might seem drastic, but can actually be the tipping point that motivates your offspring to push through pain and grow. What you do at this point can have tremendous influence. Pray for guidance.

How to Pray

A story in the Bible that strengthens my resolve is about an invalid man who had been lying on a mat near waters called the pool of Bethesda. This was a pool where people were healed when the waters stirred.

This man had been an invalid for 38 years. When Jesus saw him lying there, He asked him, "Do you want to get well?" The man told Jesus there was no one to help him get into the waters. But Jesus didn't ask him *why* he wasn't healed; He asked him if he *wanted* to be healed (John 5:5-7).

I believe with all my heart this is a key to our prayers. Pray for your mentally ill, troubled adult children to *want* to be well. Pray for them to experience a moment of clarity in realizing they are more than their illness. And pray that realization will give them the desire to be free of the confusion, depression, and darkness surrounding them.

Like the man sitting by the pool, many of our children blame others for their situation. But just as Jesus asked the man if he wanted to be well, He is asking the same of our children: "Do you want to get well?"

Even though the man blamed his problems on those around him, on their lack of help, Jesus didn't leave the man paralyzed on his mat. But He didn't help him into the water either. Jesus did not reach out His hand to help him up. Jesus said, "Get up! Pick up your mat and walk."

And that's what he did.

Dear parents, we can help our kids to get the diagnosis and prognosis they need, we can set healthy boundaries and provide a structure that can contribute to their journey toward hope and healing, and we can walk *with* them—but not *for* them.

Do what you can. Keep loving them, but trust Jesus. Pray for your child to one day pick up his mat and walk. Have faith it can happen in your child's life. It happens every day.

EFFECTIVE STRATEGY

It's important that you celebrate *every* milestone with your son or daughter, no matter how simple it might seem to you. From making that first appointment to holding a diagnosis and prognosis in hand, it's vital you let them know how proud you are of them. This is the time when buying a card of encouragement and sharing your feelings of pride is finally possible.

Chapter 9

Dangerous and Defiant

It's like my adult child has mowed a path of relationship destruction down the middle of his life. Everywhere I look I see angry and hurt people who have been used, abused, and cast aside. He has alienated everyone around him, family and friends alike. He has zero respect for me, and it makes me cry when he yells and swears at me. I didn't raise him that way. I feel like I'm the only person left who cares about him, but his temper is beginning to scare me. What should I do?

Not too long ago, I became alarmed at how many of my Facebook group members were dealing with verbally and physically abusive adult children. And even more alarmed as I learned how long it had been going on in many cases.

As parents of troubled adult children, we struggle to reconcile the little children we knew and loved with the challenging (and often unrecognizable) adult children they have become. As parents in pain, many of us have developed our own dysfunctional coping mechanisms to shield our hearts and distort the truth.

The offspring many of us interact with have been this way for a long time, and many are decidedly getting worse. Their past or present substance abuse, combined with varying degrees of emotional and/or mental illness, has significantly altered their thinking and behavior.

These are not the precious little boys and girls we raised and nurtured.

At this point, it does no good whatsoever trying to figure out what we did or didn't do right during their formative years. Casting blame or fault at this juncture is a moot point.

How should we respond when the actions of our troubled adult children begin to frighten us and threaten our own safety, or the safety of someone we love? No matter what parenting mistakes we may have made in the past, there is nothing, absolutely *nothing*, that makes it okay for your adult child to...

...lie to, cheat, or steal from you,

...verbally beat you up with vile and disgusting words or threats,

...become increasingly argumentative and dangerously defiant,

...destroy or threaten to destroy your personal property, or

...physically abuse or threaten to physically harm you or someone in your household in any way, shape, or form.

I'm acutely aware that many of our adult kids need help—a great deal of help. And while I pray for their safety and healing, my goal is to help *you* make different and better choices.

Nothing is going to change if we don't.

Opening Our Eyes

The following might be a painful exercise. Carefully read the list of personality traits and ask yourself this question: "Does my adult child possess any of these traits?" Be honest. You are doing no one, least of all your adult child, any favors by sugarcoating the painful reality. If you are unable to be objective, ask someone close to the situation to help. However, don't get angry with the person if he or she tells you things you don't want to hear. Keep your notebook nearby and write down the thoughts that come to mind as you read these traits.

1. *Irresponsibility*—repeated failure to fulfill or honor obligations and commitments, such as not paying bills, defaulting on loans, performing sloppy work, being absent or late to work, failing to honor contractual agreements.

2. *Failure to accept responsibility for own actions*—reflected

in low conscientiousness, an absence of dutifulness, antagonistic manipulation, denial of responsibility, and an effort to manipulate others through this denial.

3. *Lack of realistic, long-term goals*—an inability or persistent failure to develop and execute long-term plans and goals; a nomadic existence, aimless, lacking direction in life.

4. *Impulsivity*—the occurrence of behaviors that are unpremeditated and lack reflection or planning; inability to resist temptation, frustrations, and urges; a lack of deliberation without considering the consequences; foolhardy, rash, unpredictable, erratic, and reckless.

5. *Superficial charm*—the tendency to be smooth, engaging, charming, and slick. Not in the least shy, self-conscious, or afraid to say anything; never gets tongue-tied, and has freed himself from the social conventions about taking turns in talking, for example; often very articulate and can be extremely well-mannered when he wants to be.

6. *Grandiose self-worth*—a grossly inflated view of one's abilities and self-worth, self-assured, opinionated, cocky, a braggart; an arrogant person who believes he is a superior human being.

7. *Parasitic lifestyle*—an intentional, manipulative, selfish, and exploitative financial dependence on others as reflected in a lack of motivation, low self-discipline, and inability to begin or complete responsibilities.

8. *Poor behavioral controls*—expressions of irritability, annoyance, impatience, threats, aggression, and verbal abuse; inadequate control of anger and temper; acting hastily.

9. *Need for stimulation (proneness to boredom)*—an excessive need for novel, thrilling, and exciting stimulation; taking chances and doing things that are risky; often has low self-discipline in carrying tasks through to completion because he gets bored easily.

10. *Pathological lying*—can be moderate or high; in moderate
    form, he will be shrewd crafty, cunning, sly, and
    clever (in extreme form, he will be deceptive, deceitful,
    underhanded, unscrupulous, manipulative, and
    dishonest).

11. *Conning and manipulativeness*—the use of deceit and
    deception to cheat, con, or defraud others for personal
    gain; distinguished from impulsivity (item 4) in the degree
    to which exploitation and callous ruthlessness is present, as
    reflected in a lack of concern for the feelings and suffering
    of others.

12. *Lack of remorse or guilt*—a lack of feelings or concern for
    the losses, pain, and suffering of others; a tendency to be
    unconcerned, dispassionate, coldhearted, and unempathic.
    This item is usually demonstrated by a disdain for one's
    victims (i.e., parents).

13. *Shallow affect*—emotional poverty or a limited range or
    depth of feelings; interpersonal coldness in spite of signs of
    open gregariousness.

14. *Callousness and lack of empathy*—a lack of feelings toward
    people in general; cold, contemptuous, inconsiderate, and
    tactless.

15. *Promiscuous sexual behavior*—a variety of brief, superficial
    relations, numerous affairs, and an indiscriminate selection
    of sexual partners; the maintenance of several relationships
    at the same time; a history of attempts to sexually
    coerce others into sexual activity or taking great pride at
    discussing sexual exploits or conquests; if a son, he may
    have fathered numerous children; if a daughter, multiple
    unplanned and unwanted pregnancies and using abortion
    as birth control.

16. *Many short-term relationships*—a lack of commitment
    to a long-term relationship reflected in inconsistent,

undependable, and unreliable commitments in life, including marital.

17. *Juvenile delinquency*—behavior problems between the ages of 13 and 18; mostly behaviors that are crimes or clearly involve aspects of antagonism, exploitation, aggression, manipulation, or a callous, ruthless tough-mindedness.

18. *Criminal versatility*—a diversity of types of criminal offenses (regardless of whether the person has been arrested or convicted for them); sometimes taking great pride at getting away with crimes.

Brace yourself, Mom and Dad. If you answered yes to several of these, you may be surprised to learn that all 18 traits are actually the "clinical traits" of someone possessing what professionals now refer to as an "antisocial personality disorder," formerly known as sociopathic behavior.

A sociopath has something wrong with his conscience—either he doesn't have one, or it's severely fragmented or corrupt. Today, politically correct psychologists often call this a "character disorder," defined typically as people who don't want to take responsibility for their own actions and lives. As with any psychological disorder, there are varying degrees to which a person is affected.

The Damage Is Already Done

Some of our kids have brain chemistry that has been severely damaged. Emotional and mental illness, combined with substance abuse and often the effects of traumatic experiences, have left imprints that have changed our kids. Sadly, some are self-absorbed narcissists and even sociopaths—void of conscience. Some of these kids are a danger to themselves—and others.

In our world today, we tend to think of these people, should we think of them at all, in terms of violence. They are serial killers, mass murderers—people who, if caught, will be imprisoned, maybe even put to death by our legal system. We seldom think of the large number of nonviolent sociopaths among us, and the number is more substantial than we think.

It's almost incomprehensible and beyond painful to think of our adult children in these terms. Yet some of us must—before it's too late.

How Can They Do This?

Most of us assume it would be impossible to live without a conscience—to have no trace of guilt, remorse, empathy, or emotion for other people. Yet people who can lie, cheat, steal, con, and manipulate with practiced ease and zero guilt do indeed exist—as do people who manage to justify taking the lives of innocent people in mass shootings.

No parent wants to think of their precious child in this frightening context, and because of that, what could be subtle signs are often overlooked. Such was the case for this mother.

> On April 20, 1999, I woke up an ordinary wife and mother, happy to be shepherding my family through the daily business of work, chores, and school. Fast-forward twenty-four hours, and I was the mother of a hate-crazed gunman responsible for the worst school shooting in history. And Dylan, my golden boy, was not only dead but a mass murderer.
>
> The disconnect was so profound that I cannot wrap my head around it…More than anything else, this is what stands out about those early days in the aftermath of Columbine: the way we were able to cling, in strange and stubborn ways, to an unreality shielding us from a truth we could not yet bear. But those contortions could not protect us for very long from the wrath of a community we had come to love, or from the emerging truth about our son.[1]

There are many reasons why our adult children have become corrupt in their thinking, behaviors, attitudes, and choices. And surely any knowledgeable parent—particularly a Christian parent—will have to acknowledge the reality and powerful influence of evil. As Christians, we understand the impact of Satan's power to corrupt and destroy a human life.

Our children, however, are not beyond our prayers. On the contrary, now is the time we must pray all the harder.

The love we feel for our children will always touch us in the most tender and vulnerable parts of our heart and soul. And it's this love that will give us the power to see things as they are—not as they were—and to take the steps, with God's help, to reframe our thinking and change our perspective. We must stop making excuses for negative and dangerous behavior and begin to hold these desperately damaged individuals accountable—with firmness and love.

No matter how dark and dangerous their world has become, we can learn how to apply effective strategies that will keep us and those we love safe. As we navigate this difficult season with our troubled—and possibly dangerous—adult children, never forget that God will always make a way when there seems to be no way.

Be Prepared

I spent many years volunteering for domestic violence shelters, often called "transitional living centers." Because I understood the terror a woman feels when she is being beaten and battered, I chose to work on the front lines when women were the most vulnerable, when time was of the essence, and when being prepared could literally mean the difference between life and death.

We prepared these women to set up bank accounts, hide money, be aware of account numbers, and save copies of critical documents at an off-site location. We helped them develop passwords, safe phrases, and even temporary identities to keep them safe—and alive.

It's horrible to think that you have to set these steps in place for a future "what-if" situation. Yet women who live with physically abusive husbands understand only too well that the "next time" will come. And it will most likely be worse than the last time.

To think of some of our children in this frightening context is almost unimaginable.

Yet to do so may mean the difference between life and death.

Remember, the person who is threatening you or a loved one is not your baby boy or girl. Drugs and mental illness have changed them. Making this critical distinction in a time of crisis is vital.

EFFECTIVE STRATEGY

Be vigilant of your surroundings and be prepared. Never ignore the intuition and feelings you have that something is "off" or "wrong." If necessary, get a restraining warrant. Change your locks and computer passwords. Protect bank accounts and guard valuables. Practice responses that might diffuse a volatile situation. Ask God to give you the strength and wisdom needed to make difficult choices that will keep you—and those you love—safe.

Chapter 10

Connecting Can Be Complicated

As we work to repair or redefine the connections we have with our troubled adult children, we may also be dealing with one or more of six stress-inducing areas that can make rebuilding the relationship significantly more challenging and complicated. You won't be surprised by any item on the list: money, incarceration, painful memories, grandchildren, family interference, and blended families. Because each of these six issues plays out differently in different circumstances with different people, I don't have any one-size-fits-all solution.

But I can assure you that whatever time you spend now thinking and praying about any of these issues that impact you will be worthwhile. Ask the Lord—who promises to give us wisdom when we ask (James 1:5)—to help you know how to address any matters relevant to your unique circumstances. When we are armed with knowledge, God's wisdom, and some specific strategies, we are better prepared to—in the power of the Spirit—do what we need to do in a given family situation. Let's get started.

#1—Love Is Not Spelled M-O-N-E-Y

"Our son was arrested again."

Those five words held so much pain as this mother continued to share...

"The legal fees, bail, and cost of setting him up—and our grandson who lived with us—after his release have wiped us out. We are taking out a second mortgage to pay off that debt, his rehab, and treatment of his recently diagnosed bipolar disorder. So much is going wrong! My husband has a heart condition and needs medical care too. We argue about finances daily. I'm torn up inside. All I ever wanted was for my son to have an easier path than we did. And now how will we retire? I can't abandon my son! But if I don't help him, who will?"

Once a mother, always a mother…We love our children with every fiber of our being, no matter the choices they make—or don't make.

And far too often—especially when our children's safety and security are threatened—those feelings send us to our checkbook or credit card, and we let our children's needs trump our own financial well-being. Whether we are on a fixed income or have abundant financial resources, a common denominator among parents of troubled adult children is the frequent flow of money from us to them. Whether it's $20 or $20,000, we will face serious consequences when we consistently come to the rescue with our checkbook.

In an article in CNBC.com, Lorie Konish wisely warned, "You might want to think twice before giving money to your adult children. It could ultimately trigger your financial ruin. It is reported that 70% of parents continue to help their adult kids after the age of 18 with everything from cell phones to house payments. And many do so without even having a conversation with their kids about it."[1] Think about it. Have you ever discussed financial accountability, planning, and budgeting with your adult child? Or does he/she think you will never run out of money? If so, what did you do to contribute to that misconception?

What Motivates Us to Give?

Diane Harris said in Forbes.com, that helping with our adult children's basic living expenses makes sense only if there is a "solid reason they can't yet fend for themselves" and that anything more is "hobbling them on the path to full-fledged adulthood."[2] Our intentions are good, but the results can be bad.

When giving or loaning money to adult children, we must first consider *our* finances. Financial guru Suze Orman advises, "Say no out of love rather than yes out of fear."[3]

Our level of commitment to our children is not only a matter of the heart. It must be a matter of the head too. Our emotional responses to the problems our kids have lead many of us to refinance our homes, deplete our 401Ks, and even file for bankruptcy. Sadly, for many of us, money has done little or nothing to effect a solution to our child's grim circumstances.

Consider the Consequences

We want our kids to be happy and healthy. When our kids are sick, either with an addiction or a diagnosed mental illness, we feel compelled to do everything we can for them. But decisions about our own financial futures must be weighed against the immediate and sometimes long-term care our troubled kids may need.

Before we make any financial commitments, we must consider the consequences. Financial and emotional burdens can hurt us not only mentally and physically, but they can also have a negative effect on our marriages and other important relationships.

And some of us find ourselves not only trying to wisely navigate a relationship with our adult children, but also caring for their children. The love we have for our grandkids is complicated by the fear we have of our adult children's unhealthy lifestyle and poor choices.

Closing the Bank of Mom and Dad

Our money must, however, stop being the life preserver that buoys up our adult children, keeping them afloat after yet another shipwreck. You and I might actually be amazed by how well our adult children can swim when given—when we give them!—the opportunity. More important, they themselves might be surprised by their ability to survive without life support—and that's a powerful lesson that no amount of money can buy.

America's Missing Male Workers

And now for an interesting statistic. Did you know that more than seven million men between the ages of 25 and 54—prime working age—have dropped out of the labor force? That means they're not only unemployed, but they have also given up looking for a job.[4]

Economist Erik Hurst at the University of Chicago suggests that video games may be luring our men out of the workforce. He found that young men without college degrees "have replaced 75 percent of the time they would have spent working with time spent on the computer, mostly playing games."[5]

One of my SANITY Facebook support group members knows this all too well. She wrote, "My 25-year-old son still doesn't have a job. I come home after work only to find him asleep or playing video games. After asking him if he had any luck finding a job today, he bristled, 'Leave me alone! You're messing up my game!'"

Erik Hurst adds, "It may be that living in virtual realities distracts men from their deeply unsatisfying lives—but it also lessens their incentive to hunt for work, take less prestigious [but available] jobs, or make big changes in their lives."[6]

Virtual reality seems as insidious an enemy as mental illness and addiction.

Addiction and Incarceration

Addiction is definitely an enemy that too often leads to another enemy and therefore can't be ignored. As my friend Judy Hampton points out, we parents do have a weapon we can wield: "We stopped the flow of money the day we realized that all the money we were giving our adult child was only underwriting sin and addiction." And, sadly, this substance abuse contributes significantly to incarceration. Look at these statistics:

- Some 12 percent of adult men have been convicted of a felony (this number does not include those currently imprisoned), and employers are understandably reluctant to hire ex-cons. Many of these men find themselves unemployable.

- It isn't clear whether pain and sickness keep people out of the workforce or if being out of work makes people sick, but nearly half of [the unemployed] report taking a pain-killer every day.

- About two-thirds of the men taking pain medication were using prescription drugs—contributing to the nationwide opioid addiction epidemic that causes 78 deaths every day, from overdoses on pills and heroin.[7]

Is our financial enabling another reason for our troubled adult children's addiction and joblessness, or are their substance abuse and unemployment the reason we enable them?

#2—The Impact of Incarceration

A woman in our Facebook group shared her heartache, one that far too many of us have experienced: "Our son and daughter have been in and out of jail a half-dozen times. Now our son will be doing time in federal prison for a drug-related crime. Our daughter is on probation with an electronic monitoring ankle bracelet and must remain no more than five feet from the front door of our house."

Her words vividly remind me of the deep anguish and fear I experienced the first time my son was arrested as an adult. An experience that has, sadly, been repeated often over the past years. It still breaks my heart to think of him being in prison. I cannot fathom a life where locks, bars, and the constant threat of violence are part of his everyday existence. And the aloneness must be paralyzing.

Waiting Together

We parents may also feel a paralyzing aloneness when we face the reality that our troubled adult child is in jail, the consequence of some bad choices and unthinking decisions. Even before they were incarcerated, many of our adult kids would withdraw and isolate themselves from us and others, and we parents are no different. In her book *Waiting Together: Hope and Healing for Families of Prisoners,* Carol Kent calls us to not isolate ourselves but, yes, to wait together:

We sometimes think there is no one in our lives who really cares, but it may be that we're just tempted to pull away from others. During the first few months following my son's arrest, it often seemed easier to pull down the window shades, to not answer the phone or emails or text messages, to try to make everyone around me think I was "fine." But I'm discovering that when I allow people to help carry my grief as I talk with them, spend time together, and open up about the tough days, my problem seems lighter. I realize I'm not alone.

That's what this book is all about—waiting *together*, instead of stubbornly trying to hide our pain and resisting the support of those people closest to us. We really do need each other![8]

Carol closes every chapter with a section called "His Words Over You." One chapter's closing was based on Ephesians 4:32 and 3:20— "Be quick to embrace love. Allow people to be kind and compassionate to you. As you open your heart, you'll discover that you're able to do immeasurably more than you could ever imagine."

Wait together. We need each other.

Finding Inspiration

When we do choose to wait together, we can find ourselves inspired and encouraged. That happens to me even through letters and emails from parents of incarcerated adult children. This email is an example:

> *Hi! I read your book* Setting Boundaries with Your Adult Children, *and it saved me! My daughter is 21, an addict, and in jail for six months. She hasn't lived with me for two years, a difficult boundary that needed to be set. For a while she was homeless. Now she says she's the only "indigent in jail." She wants money for the commissary, but this shouldn't be a comfortable situation! I said to her, "I'm sorry, but I have my own bills to pay and cannot take care of yours too." I have not given her money, but I have sent books and I write letters. I want her*

to know I love her, but that love isn't spelled m-o-n-e-y. Thank
you for your books, knowledge, faith, and strength.

Inspiring and encouraging, right?

Sharing our stories requires us to draw closer to each other. Sharing our stories also gives us perspective, strength, and comfort as we hear other people's stories. We learn that life is hard for everyone, and at some point we may realize that some of the greatest advances in history were made by someone who went through great pain and hardship.

What if the apostle Paul's mother had taken her exhausted and overworked son's place on that Damascus Road in order to save him a trip? Or what if Esther had never gone to the palace but instead convinced her well-meaning uncle to let her stay home and catch up on her shows? What if Beethoven's mother had determined that composing music was too stressful for her deaf adult son? What if their parents or other relatives had kept these people from living out their destiny?

I have another question: What if the trials and tribulations your adult child is presently going through are intended to teach him a valuable lesson that will change the entire course of his life—and the lives of future generations? What if, like Paul, your adult child needs to experience the pain of prison—either concrete or intangible—to fulfill her life purpose? And what if the incarceration of our troubled adult children is intended to teach them God's mercy and to show them His purpose in His plan?

People from all walks of life have often changed the course of history after and even because of some disastrous life experiences. If their moms and dads had continually come to their rescue and kept them from experiencing the pain, the outcome of those children's lives would have been radically different.

Pain often fuels purpose.

#3—When the Past Haunts the Present

For many of us, our painful memories and negative thinking began in childhood and continued over time. We've been abandoned, abused, neglected, molested, bullied, and bruised. We were underachievers or overachievers, trying to fit in or never fitting in. We've struggled with inferiority, insecurity, and identity. We've made choices we're ashamed of and mistakes we regret. We've lost parents, siblings, spouses, and children to death or self-destruction. We've suffered the devastation of divorce. We've been betrayed and bewildered by people we trusted. We've had wayward children, grandchildren, and siblings. And we've fought depression, anxiety, disabilities, and a host of mental health and emotional issues.

Our life experiences have left lasting damage and heartache. We have been scarred by abusive relationships, and our own children have verbally and physically injured us. Our loved ones suffer with PTSD after serving their country in the military, and for some, incarceration has left wounds that may never heal. Emotional wounds, illness, serious accidents, and even past medical procedures have scarred us, leaving deep gashes as reminders. We wallow in guilt, and we comfort ourselves by blaming others. Haunted by the past, we withdraw in disillusionment, depression, and despair.

Violated Boundaries

When our boundaries are violated physically, verbally, sexually, or emotionally, the way we see our world, the way we process information, and the ways we communicate with others are forever changed. And the younger we are when the abuse happens, the more intense the long-term effects. Too easily, young people can get horribly lost in the ramifications of the trauma and their memories of those events. In fact, many theories suggest that childhood trauma increases one's risk for psychological disorders in adulthood, including post-traumatic stress disorder, depression, and substance abuse.

Healing the Past with a Renewed Mind

When we've been scarred by painful experiences, we develop coping mechanisms to protect ourselves. Sometimes, the methods we adopt help us overcome intrusive memories; other times, they only mask the memory temporarily; and in some cases, the methods we use are more harmful than helpful in our relationships. This can be especially true when boundaries of any kind were violated.

Violated boundaries can be extremely painful and very slow to heal. But we can find some healing and relief from the past that haunts us when we take responsibility for our thoughts and make the intentional choice to replace our negative thinking with something better, healthier, loving, truthful, and hopeful. Sometimes we find relief when we drag the skeletons in the closet out into the light of day, confront them head-on, and thereby destroy their power. We must do what we can to stop allowing our past to impact our present and determine the course of our future. We can rest in the truth that our good Shepherd will guide us to healing pastures and refreshing water.

#4—Grandchildren Caught in the Cross Fire

When we are taking care of our grandchildren, either temporarily or permanently, we will find ourselves providing for them financially. In some cases, this new expense may be a burden to our already stretched finances. If you are in that position currently, visit my website for updated resources that may help.

Across the United States, more than 13 million children are living with their grandparents.[9] Our nation's opioid epidemic is a factor. Our troubled adult children may be self-medicating, or addiction has caused mental illness. Whatever their stories, our adult children are unable to care for their children—and many of them do have children.

Whether our troubled adult children are incarcerated, involved in criminal activity, unemployed, or emotionally and mentally ill, we must act. Our grandchildren's lives truly hang in the balance.

According to Brandon Gaille's article "23 Statistics on Grandparents Raising Grandchildren":

> 2.5 million grandparents every day are taking on the responsibilities required to raise these children. That doesn't mean there aren't other relatives in the picture that are providing support, but there are 1 million kids today that have their grandparents as their sole parental influences while growing up.[10]

That puts a lot of pressure on the older shoulders of Grandma and Grandpa.

Here are some facts about children who are raised by grandparents:

- Custodial grandchildren have higher levels of behavioral and emotional problems than children in the average US population.

- Boys raised by grandparents are more likely to have externalized behavioral problems than girls, who are more likely to internalize issues.

- One-fifth of grandparents have incomes below the poverty line.[11]

If You Want to Adopt Your Grandchild (Legalities)

Adoption means taking complete and permanent responsibility for your grandchild and eliminating the possibility of legal interference by the birth parents. Adoption shouldn't be considered if the child may reunite with his/her birth parents someday, or if you—the grandparent or relative—can only care for the child temporarily.

You need to know this as well: To adopt a child, the birth parents' rights must be terminated. Then an adoption application needs to be filed with the probate court along with an agreement of adoption. Child Protective Services will investigate and determine whether the applicant would be a good adoptive parent. If the child is 12 or older, he or she must agree to be adopted.[12]

Every state maintains its own laws concerning adoption. AARP has a "State Fact Sheet for Grandparents and Other Relatives Raising Children" available online at its website, http://www.aarp.org/relation ships/friends-family/grandfacts-sheets/. Be sure you do your research.

It's our responsibility to be the best grandparents we can be, but we won't be if fear and guilt guide our decisions. Gaining permanent custody of your grandchildren may not be the best option for you or for them. Approach this decision with much prayer, much thought, and much godly counsel.

Get Support

You saw the statistic: If you are already raising your grandchildren, you aren't alone, so don't go it alone! Websites, Facebook groups, and community groups can offer support, direction, and encouragement, and Grandparentingblog.com is chockful of wisdom.

Remember, you need community. The *A* step in SANITY is especially important: ASSEMBLE support. Reach out for help. Ask people to pray. Don't be too proud to let your church and friends know what you need. Always hold on to hope for your grandchildren to one day either be reunited with their parents or for God to provide another family, the best family for your grandchild.

#5—Family Interference

In his book *Don't Let Your Kids Kill You,* Charles Rubin addresses a painful topic that many of my readers experience: the interference of someone else as they navigate the choppy waters caused by their troubled adult children. The interference can be instigated by the adult children themselves when their parents start enforcing healthy boundaries and cut off financial support. Rubin observes that:

> [even] a distant relative who has never even seen the addict but is nevertheless a blood relation [will be approached for money]…Hardly ever is the addict turned away point blank. Often, it only takes one phone call from the addict explaining his or her dilemma with "cruel, unfeeling parents," for the now-outraged distant relative to lend this "child victim" immediate financial support and to bombard the parents with phone calls and letters demanding that they do the same.[13]

As if receiving those phone calls wouldn't be infuriating enough, Rubin goes on to report this:

> In many cases, these well-meaning but misguided people fail to investigate anything further than what the addict has told them. From my experience, they almost never ask the

parents' side of the story. Mostly, they just leap into the picture, assuming the role of rescuer. Their interference in situations that don't concern them winds up doing far more harm than good.

So convincing is the addict that any defense on the parents' part is often seen as suspicious, especially when the parent is feeling outraged by the intrusion. Emotional outbursts by the parents merely confirm to the "rescuer" what the addict has already indicated, that the parent has an unbridled temper, is unstable, and obviously wants to unload the kids on the side of the road.[14]

As if trying to connect with a troubled adult child isn't difficult enough, we also may find ourselves the target of friendly fire.

When Grandparents Interfere

I received a letter from a one-time enabling mom who was beginning to find some sanity in her relationship with her 19-year-old drug-addicted daughter. She and her husband had worked shoulder to shoulder as they established some difficult but much-needed boundaries. They began with the S step in SANITY: They *STOPPED the flow of money*. Sadly, the plan they implemented was subverted by her own parents. The second paragraph in her lengthy email broke my heart—and I'm sad to say it's not an isolated incident:

> *We have pretty much set up and stood by our boundaries. Just last month we stopped most financial support... Well, my daughter ended up moving in with my parents. To be honest, I was relieved at first because I knew she would be safe. But I didn't think things through.*
>
> *Now we had to set some boundaries with my parents because they expected financial support from us. I still feel guilty about this, because they do not have a lot to give, but my daughter has a job. I explained she should pay them rent. Instead, my parents have become the enabling grandparents.*

> *My daughter…manipulates my parents, and I feel guilty that*
> *the chaos that was once in our house is now in theirs. My dad*
> *is fed up, but my mom refuses to see the truth.*

This is a tough situation. What do you do when other family members interfere? When you and your spouse are finally in agreement about parenting your troubled adult child, but your adult child's grandparents aren't? What do you do when they step into the enabling role you have finally stepped out of?

If possible, ask them to go to a counseling session with you. A counselor will explain the importance of the steps you've taken. Give them my book *Setting Boundaries with Your Adult Children,* and ask them to read it. Try to help them understand that you want the very best for your daughter, but you've realized that means letting her hit rock bottom. Have an honest conversation. Thank them for their help, but explain that you've tried all they're now doing, and it didn't help. Continuing to speak the truth in love, let the grandparents know they are actually hurting your daughter rather than helping her.

And don't forget to pray for their eyes to be open to see their granddaughter's manipulation for what it is.

#6—Blended Families

Our final stress-inducing situation that makes establishing a healthy relationship with our troubled adult children difficult is that of a blended family.

According to StepFamily.org, blended families are more the norm today than the original mother, father, and child version. Look at these statistics from the U.S. Census Bureau:

- 1300 new stepfamilies are forming every day.
- Over 50% of US families are remarried or re-coupled.
- The average marriage in America lasts only seven years.
- One out of two marriages ends in divorce.
- 75% remarry.

- 66% of those living together or remarried break up when children are involved.

- 80% of remarried, or re-coupled, partners with children are two-career families.

- 50% of the 60 million children under the age of 13 are currently living with one biological parent and that parent's current partner.[15]

Blended families bring a whole new dynamic into families dealing with troubled adult children. When both parties marry for a second time, children and adult children are often involved. It's therefore imperative to discuss before marrying how you will handle not only the kids, but also the kid crises that will come. The big question the new husband and the new wife need to address is, "Who comes first—the kids or the marriage?"

Time and time again, the kids get first place, leaving the spouse to pick up the leftovers. Talk about the children you both bring into the family. Be clear about expectations. If you've already said your vows and now, ten years later, a troubled adult child has wreaked havoc in your marriage, it's not too late to start the conversation.

If an adult child is shredding your marriage, I encourage you to seek marital counseling. Work together to once again put your marriage first. After that, the two of you can work toward the health of the troubled adult (step)child.

When Parenting Is the Problem

Growing up with an alcoholic father, Sophia always felt that she was a reason he drank:

> As an adult I finally realized that his drinking was his problem, but it affected the whole family. Children should not have to walk on eggshells. They are to be nurtured, protected, and provided with safety, security, and—most important—love. If that isn't happening, someone needs to intervene and advocate for the children and their well-being. The addicts are oblivious to the damage they are doing to their children.

If we suspect that our troubled adult children are neglecting or emotionally or physically abusing their children, it is our responsibility to call the local authorities or Child Protective Services.

Keeping Our SANITY

Parenting may truly be the most difficult job in the world, but parenting troubled adult children is that difficult job on steroids. Money issues, incarceration, painful memories, grandchildren, family interference, and blended families—these circumstances of life as well as consequences of our troubled children's choices and decisions further increase the level of difficulty of parenting in general and of connecting with our children in particular.

Our perspective on the situation as well as how we respond to our troubled adult children and their mental illness can have a profound effect on the relationship we share with them. We must tread carefully and be aware of our influence to build up or tear down. When our motives come from a place of love, miraculous things can—and do—happen.

EFFECTIVE STRATEGY

Search your own heart and ask God to reveal ways you can show His love to your son or daughter with your words and your actions. Also ask God to show you how to speak hope into your child's life. Then, remembering that Jesus is Emmanuel, "God with us," write in your journal a personalized version of this prayer—or the parts of this prayer you find most meaningful—because we all have moments when the only thing we can do is pray:

> Lord, I confess that I have made mistakes as a parent. In an honest desire to give (name) the things I did not have as a child, I overindulged him/her. Fearful of damaging his/her spirit, I failed to exercise healthy discipline. Sadly, these actions have nurtured an arrogant and disrespectful adult with a rebellious, self-serving, and self-destructive nature.

Because of my failure to properly teach and demonstrate to (name) that there are serious consequences for wrong actions, I have inadvertently given the enemy a comfortable place to live and rule in (name's) heart. Although I wish I had recognized what I was doing sooner, I will not resign myself to the way things are. I have faith that change is possible.

Today, in the name of Jesus and by the transformative power of Christ, I rebuke this enemy of rebellion and disobedience. I will no longer turn a blind eye to my adult child's unacceptable—and often sinful—behavior. I also refuse to be held captive by his/her volatile emotions.

God, please help me to—from now on—consistently respond to (name's) poor choices with firmness and love and in ways that bring glory and honor to You. Give me the words to assure (name) of my love for him/her, that I love the sinner but hate the sin.

I will no longer live in bondage to past mistakes, and I come to You now with a humble, repentant, and teachable spirit. I pray for Your forgiveness—and I ask You to help me forgive my daughter/son. I pray, too, that in Your power and with Your love, (name) will join me in this place and commit our relationship to You for healing and direction. Amen.

Chapter 11

Connecting Needs to Be Compassionate

Our need for connection begins the moment we are born, and that need is first fulfilled by the people closest to us—those feeding us, holding us, caring for us. When we have been those nurturers, we find a break with the children we brought into the world devastating. It's painful to watch harmful patterns of behavior emerge in our children, have communication break down, and see them turn away. We may desperately seek to find ways to fix these broken connections, but rarely is there any positive result. Instead, we often end up circling the mountain of codependency (the dysfunctional helping relationship where one person supports or enables another person's drug addiction, alcoholism, gambling addiction, poor mental health, immaturity, irresponsibility, or underachievement), holding our children with a tighter and tighter grip. Of course, this approach doesn't make for any genuine or positive connection.

If we want the dynamics of our relationship with our children to change, we must be willing to connect with our sons and daughters in completely different ways than we have in the past.

Creating healthy connections begins when we communicate authentically and rationally rather than emotionally. After all, most of our kids are used to us freaking out and reacting emotionally. Our choice to speak and respond calmly and rationally can be a real game changer.

That's why our goal in this chapter is to learn how to improve the way we communicate with our adult children. To show them more love and compassion and less anger and judgment. In some cases, this switch will require a Herculean effort because our children's decisions have broken our hearts and drained our bank accounts. After all we've done for them, they have never seemed grateful.

Thankfully, we have an example we can follow as we learn to communicate differently.

You may know the story: After all God did to set the Israelites free from bondage in Egypt, they somehow failed to remember all the miracles He had performed on their behalf. In fact, while Moses was on Mount Sinai speaking to God about His guidelines and plans for the people of Israel, they got tired of waiting and, acting in sin and rebellion, built a calf of gold that they worshipped and celebrated. Behaving like spoiled, ungrateful children, the Israelites deserved to be punished for their arrogance and disobedience, but how did God respond to their behavior? God did not desert or disown His people. Instead, He responded according to His nature: He is "a forgiving God, gracious and compassionate, slow to anger and abounding in love" (Nehemiah 9:17).

Compassion is the key.

Compassion can help us break the unhealthy patterns of the past and connect with our troubled adult children in a new way. Let me tell you of one woman who has forged some positive connections with her adult daughter even though her child's decisions still bring heartache.

Susan and her husband had one son when they decided to adopt a baby girl they named Caitlin. Their family now seemed complete and was happy...until Caitlin's early teens. That's when the trouble started—rebellion, disobedience, a bipolar diagnosis, and eventually drug use. Susan and her husband tried everything to help Caitlin along the way, from direct orders to groundings, from negative reinforcement to counseling and medication, and even a long stay in a faith-based rehab camp for troubled teens. Every step Caitlin took forward was followed by multiple steps backward and frequent relapses. Even after Caitlin turned 18, her parents still tried to fix the next problem and the next and the next. Finally, through compassionate self-examination, a stronger foundation of faith, and much prayer, Susan and her husband decided to jump off the gerbil wheel of insanity. In applying the *S* step of SANITY, they were able to STOP their usual responses, adopt a hands-off policy, and trust their adult daughter and her ongoing bad decisions to God. Caitlin's parents discovered peace they never thought would come without their daughter's full recovery. And in the wake of this decision to step back from Caitlin, they watched God work miracles in their daughter's life.

Things aren't perfect for Susan's family, but they are moving in the direction of greater trust in God and in one another. They live close enough to Caitlin to lend support when needed and appropriate, but they are far enough away for Caitlin to have an independent life.

Susan and her husband found that it was possible to change the connection with their adult daughter by operating from compassion instead of relating to their daughter primarily out of obligation and fear for their daughter's health, safety, and well-being.

A Hopeful Connection

Our relationships with our adult children can be characterized by various emotional bonds, and those bonds usually fall into one of two opposing categories: love and trust, or fear and guilt. Let's first consider trust.

To begin creating healthy connections, you must be brutally honest with yourself as you take stock of your relationship with your child. What emotions rise to the top when you think about that relationship? Parental love is usually present, so you will likely start there. No one would question whether or not you love your child, but is trust a part of your relationship? Do you no longer trust your child—or has your child stopped trusting you?

And what about your love for your son or daughter? Do you—acting in love—step back and allow your child to experience the consequences of wrong choices, or do you act emotionally and respond to his or her poor choices by rescuing and protecting? Generally, whenever we seek to protect, "fix," or rescue our troubled child, we are not operating out of love, but out of fear, guilt, anger, or perhaps even obligation. But interacting with our children out of these negative emotions will do neither them nor us any good.

So what impact is your love having on your child? Are you encouraging healthy independence, or are you fostering unhealthy dependence? Do you speak hope into your child's life, or have you given up that things will ever change?

To connect out of pure love rather than fear means we may need to watch our children suffer. This is hard. But God has a plan "to prosper...and not to harm [your child]" (Jeremiah 29:11).

This promise reflects God's character and heart for our troubled kids and for us. The word *prosper* is the word *shalom* in Hebrew, and *shalom* means "peace, wholeness, and prosperity." God's plan for our kids, then, is peace, wholeness, and victory over their demons, both physical and psychological.

Hold on to this hope—and don't hesitate to share it with your child.

A New Connection

In some cases, building a healthy connection may require us to demolish an unhealthy one—like the connection that comes when we are enablers.

One of the most crippling wrong connections we have with our troubled children is enabling them to avoid responsibilities and escape the consequences of their actions. Rather than helping them grow into productive and responsible adults, we make it easier for them to become much less responsible. We are enablers.

An enabler notices a negative pattern of behavior yet continues to allow—to enable—the person to persist in his unhealthy actions. Simply put, a parent's enabling provides opportunities for adult children to comfortably continue their unacceptable behavior. This scenario is never good for child or parent.

Sadly, though, the line between acceptable and unacceptable behavior is blurry for many enabling parents. Not only may we be unaware of what it means to enable—and that's often the case—but we're equally fuzzy about what is acceptable behavior and what isn't. It should, for instance, be unacceptable for a child to borrow the family car with a full tank of gas and return it on empty and without any intention of paying for the fuel she used. It should be unacceptable for an adult child living at home to sleep all day, stay up all night playing video games, and leave a mess in the kitchen for someone else to clean up. It should also be unacceptable behavior for an adult child to scream and swear at a parent or sibling, no matter what mental illness he is dealing with.

When we parents continue to allow behaviors like these, we are establishing, if not reinforcing, a pattern with our children that will be hard to break. When we allow their inappropriate behavior to occur again and again—when we accept behavior that should be unacceptable and allow bad habits to take root and even thrive—our enabling eventually becomes as natural to many of us as breathing. All the while, though, a nagging feeling deep in our hearts and souls tells us that something very wrong is happening.

Yet, accepting unacceptable behavior seems to be standard operating procedure for many parents of troubled adult children. Why do you suppose that's the case?

Far too often, it's because we haven't stopped to apply the *N* step in SANITY, which is "NIP Excuses in the Bud." Enabling parents have an uncanny ability to make excuses for troubled kids.

We make excuses for their anger, disrespect, lying, cheating, stealing, verbal abuse, property damage, laziness, and additional actions we would never accept from anyone else. Yes, many of our sons and daughters are struggling with serious issues, but that is no excuse for their negative behavior or for us to tolerate, much less enable, it.

Does any part of this discussion of enabling resonate in your spirit? Grab your notebook and make a list of your child's behaviors you think should be unacceptable—and some of them may be actions you've tolerated far too long. If your child is living with you, add these items to the Residential Agreement contract you're going to develop. If your child lives elsewhere, plan to discuss these items at some point.

Troubled children can and should be held accountable for their actions, and there are appropriate ways to do so within the confines of their emotional or mental illness.

So, if you recognize yourself as an enabler—and that may be hard to admit—you may be contributing significantly to your adult child's inappropriate behavior.

It's time to apply the *S* step in SANITY.

STOP.

Listening with an Open Heart

We've all heard that there's a reason why we have two ears and one mouth. Even though we chuckle when we read those words, we know we need the reminder to listen twice as much as we speak.

You may have heard these words from the apostle James: "Everyone should be quick to listen, slow to speak and slow to become angry" (James 1:19). The word *quick* means "to be ready." Most of us tend to be very ready to give a piece of our mind or our side of the story. It can be difficult to be ready and willing to listen.

So take a deep breath…and listen first.

To strengthen your resolve, think about how many times you have regretted the words you spoke when you lashed out in anger or frustration. Many of us have damaged or even lost a good relationship with a family member or friend because we spoke before we listened.

There's so much more to listening, though, than meets the ear. Real listening reaches beyond the words spoken; real listening involves hearing the speaker's heart. Oh, we can *hear* our kids explain their behavior, but may we choose to actively *listen* for their pain. Effective listening does more than merely hear sounds.

To be honest, it has taken me quite a while to learn to listen to my son with my ears, eyes, and heart—and to listen for his heart. The more intentional I am about this, the more I'm able to perceive the critical nuances of his emotional and mental illness symptoms.

I distinctly recall a time a few years back, shortly after Chris had been released from prison. He was staying with me in Texas, and we went to a Walmart Supercenter. The store was exceptionally crowded that day, and both the noise and activity level were high. My son has a very stoic nature—he doesn't whine or complain much—but within a few minutes, his eyes began to dart around, sweat broke out on his forehead, and his breathing became fast and shallow. He tried to walk alongside me as I pushed the cart, but within a few minutes he gently put his hand on my arm, and I could feel him shaking.

"Mom, can I please have your keys? I need to go sit in the car and wait for you…This is too much."

His cornflower blue eyes looked frightened, even desperate. Clearly, the noise and activity had triggered panic in his psyche, and his fight-or-flight instinct had kicked in. I didn't tell him to try to get a grip; I didn't downplay in any way what he was feeling. I reached into my purse for my keys and handed them to him. I had to do this often. Being in any crowded place was painful for him.

Chris's PTSD (post-traumatic stress disorder) is an insidious condition that rears its ugly head at the most inopportune times, often forcing Chris to isolate himself until he gets it under control. I try so hard to understand it, but I don't always succeed.

Parents, we must remember that many of our children have an illness we cannot see. Trying to force them to function like a "normal" adult never works. And downplaying their anxiety or fear—because we don't understand it—will never help us connect with our child.

Again, when someone we care about is struggling with emotional or mental illness, our ability to treat him with love, grace, and compassion is critical for his healing. But sometimes extending love, grace, and compassion is hard for us parents to do, particularly if we are still struggling to forgive our children for things they have done and the damage and the hurt they have caused.

With God's help, though, we can learn to listen—not just hear—and then respond in ways that foster hope and bring healing to our hearts *and* to the hearts of those we love. Connecting with troubled adult children isn't just about changes *they* need to make. It's very much about changes *we* need to make.

Listening with Compassion

As parents, we often go into discipline mode or teaching mode.

Both are important parental roles, but if we fail to add a compassion mode, our adult children may lose their willingness or desire to communicate with us. If we punish their honesty with quick words and anger, or if we respond to situations like a teacher would respond to a pupil, we may burn the bridge to healthy communication entirely. Sadly, that's where many parents find themselves today.

But it's never too late to build a new bridge, to form a new and better connection with our adult children.

When we're in compassion mode as we listen—when we listen before we speak, advise, or respond in any way—we show our adult kids that we care. Furthermore, as Christians, we have the Holy Spirit to enable us to hear beyond the sound waves to our child's heart and motives. The Spirit will give us the wisdom we need when we stop, ask, and listen.

In some cases the Spirit may bring to mind Proverbs 15:1—"A gentle answer turns away wrath." Case in point...

The mother of a friend of mine was teaching kindergarten children in the Bronx. The children were unruly and disrespectful, and they never listened. Desperate one day, the teacher cried out to God: "How can I teach these children?" His response was, "Whisper."

From that day on, she only spoke to the class in a very soft voice. The children began to listen and obey. Other teachers were amazed by the class's transformation.

Ask the Lord to help you listen before you say anything and then to show you how to respond. He might want you to whisper.

A Spiritual Connection

Many of our troubled adult children have retreated into their pain rather than pushing through it and coming out on the other side stronger and wiser. They've allowed circumstances to beat them up, tear them down, or imprison them, either mentally, emotionally, or literally. They haven't considered how these same trials could stretch them in ways that would develop their character, prove their mettle, and give them a sense of achievement.

Actually, many adult children have no idea what they're truly capable of accomplishing. For various reasons—lack of confidence, fear of failing, fear of the unknown—they've never really tried to move ahead with confidence and be all they can be. Let's encourage our adult children to identify their dreams, set goals, and begin to hope for those possibilities to become realities.

We want our children to have bright futures, even if that dream seems distant or impossible. We want to impact and influence their lives so that they can change their path, their attitude, and their trajectory. The hope that our faith would impact our children is one reason why we must stand strong in our trust that God will keep His great promises regarding our trials and our children's future.

God's Word guides, strengthens, and empowers us. In fact, Drs. Cloud and Townsend take the position that knowing God's Word is vital for all growth:

> The Bible teaches everything that people need to grow. All the principles and truth necessary for spiritual growth and for relating to God and others, maturing and working out personal issues and problems have been provided. God did not begin maturing people only in the twentieth century. He has been leading, healing, and growing his flock ever since he created us. This is why we view all personal growth as spiritual growth, whether it be religious, emotional, relational, or behavioral.[1]

Parenting can help us become faithful pray-ers and committed Bible students, and one result will be personal growth and, therefore, much spiritual growth. We will grow as we reach out with compassion to our adult children. The process will be a lesson in personal growth, a lesson that takes time. There is so much pain to overcome, so many words and actions to forgive, so much sin to confess, so many decisions to be made. And this is true for everyone. But our choice to fix our eyes on Jesus and to rely on the Word of God will guide and empower us every step of the way—even when we can't see what that next step is.

Spiritual Fruit

With my dyslexia and ADD, my brain sometimes has a tough time remembering things. That's why I'm big on acronyms, mnemonic devices, and word pictures. Over the past few years, I've developed what I think is a rather useful word picture exercise that helps me to communicate better with my son—particularly when every fiber of my being wants to scream or shake some sense into him. (I never said I was perfect.)

You might find this exercise helpful as well.

I've been praying for years for God to help me *respond rationally* rather than *react emotionally* to my son, to have self-control when I'm confronted with his unhealthy actions and behavior. I'm getting better at responding with grace, but it can still be a struggle. I'm not ashamed to admit that many times my internal voice is screaming, *Seriously?! You did WHAT?!*

But then I remember the *S* step in SANITY, and I STOP myself.

And then I think about throwing fruit at him. That's right. Fruit.

Fellow parents, to reach out to our kids with compassion means to communicate with love. We must speak hope over our hopeless children. We must listen with kindness and compassion. Our troubled kids will not hear a word we say if it's spoken out of anger or judgment. Of course, there are times when this is really, *really* hard to do. That's when calling upon the Spirit of God to help us obey the Word of God can change us—and hopefully, He will use our example and His power to change our children as well.

So when I throw (invisible) fruit at my son's head, I'm consciously thinking about the fruit God gives us when we walk in His will and according to His Word. I'm thinking about the fruit of the Spirit— "love, joy, peace, forbearance, kindness, goodness, faithfulness, gentleness and self-control" (Galatians 5:22-23)—which is fruit He wants us to share with others.

The next time you're ready to lose your cool, throw fruit instead.

It works.

A Vision of Our Child's Deliverance

I recently heard a woman in her fifties share a beautiful story of healing from bipolar disorder. Beth's bipolar was so severe she could not cook, clean, take care of her children, or keep a job. On many days, she considered suicide, but by God's grace she never acted upon those thoughts.

As Beth tells the story of her battle for healing, she weaves a narrative of how God gave her a vision for victory. He showed her that one day she would be free of the fear, depression, manic mood swings, and suicidal thoughts.

Beth's healing did come, the result of a process that began with first getting a professional diagnosis. That was followed by medication, seeking God, forgiving others, and believing in the miracle. When she shares her story, she encourages others to write down a vision of their deliverance. She held onto this promise for many years: "Do not be afraid. Stand firm and you will see the deliverance the LORD will bring you today…The LORD will fight for you; you need only to be still" (Exodus 14:13-14).

I encourage you to, like Beth, put your hope in God—in His goodness, faithfulness, and love for you and your child—*and* expect Him to work. Also pray and ask God to give you a vision of a healed child and a healed relationship with him or her.

We know that through Christ our sons and daughters can find not only healing, but also courage, strength, confidence, and compassion. We should also remember that many of our children first see Christ when they see Him flowing through us. When they receive His love and His compassion from us.

Reach Out with Respect

As we conclude this chapter, I feel compelled to discuss a topic related to our extending compassion to our adult children. That topic is respect.

Now, I understand how frightening and dangerous it can be when adult children struggle with a substance abuse disorder, and those drugs turn them into strangers.

But in our desire to help or even rescue, many of us have violated not only our children's privacy but their basic rights as well. We've ransacked their rooms, gone through their cell phone records, and checked their text messages. We've gone through their wallets and purses; we've even checked their pockets. We are obsessed with both knowing what they're up to and changing their behavior.

One mom writes, "Before I loan him money for medication he claims he needs, I must have confirmation from his doctors that he even has an illness. I have asked him for proof for years. I need his medical records or even a phone call from his team of doctors telling me he truly is sick. I have searched his home, his phone, and his car for evidence that he has appointments and prescriptions. Until I see proof, I am not going to help him with another thing."

This mom is obviously frustrated. Her desire to have proof before extending further help is understandable and advisable, but the way she is going about it won't help her build a strong connection with her son. Her approach will not foster accountability and trust.

Many parents of troubled adult children have gone through their belongings. It's one thing when we're concerned about their safety, and they are young, underage, and living in our home. It's another thing entirely to treat an adult like a child.

Yes, it's quite possible that this frustrated mother's son doesn't want money for prescribed medications. He could have any number of reasons for wanting that money, including the purchase of illegal drugs. I've read several email exchanges between this mother and her son, and most read like a playground shouting match between two bratty kids. This son doesn't live at home, he's in his midtwenties, and his mother uses money and negative control as a way to stay connected to him. That is never a good approach.

Parents, I understand how frustrated you are. How fearful you are. And how angry. I understand that some of your children are in the throes of addiction and still using, and others are suffering from antisocial personality disorders or psychotic behavior and cannot be trusted. Some are incarcerated. Still others have no concept of truth. They can weave a web of lies and skillfully manipulate you into believing them even when instincts tell you not to.

All of this makes protecting yourself by any means possible quite understandable and even necessary. So you justify the illegal search and seizure of property. Parents, please hear me out: *You do not have a legal right to search the belongings of your adult child* just because you want proof of illness or addiction or if you suspect nefarious actions.

If, however, your troubled adult child is living with you and has a known history of drug use or criminal behavior, it is well within your rights to make periodic routine searches of his or her property. In fact, make this be a mandatory requirement in the signed residential housing contract you have with your child.

Should you find contraband in your house, you must be prepared to immediately follow up with the established consequences set forth in the contract. If you don't have a signed contract, create one as soon as possible. (See Appendix A at the back of this book for a template.).

Finally, remember our goal as Christian parents: to grow spiritually as we walk in God's will and according to His Word and to exhibit the character of Christ in all we do. And God Himself will help us do this.

EFFECTIVE STRATEGY

No matter their struggles, our sons and daughters need to be treated like people, not problems. In addition to having food, clothing, and a place to live, our children also need purpose and hope. So consider ways to communicate with your child that might lead to a discussion about his or her goals and dreams—and listen.

Chapter 12

The Power of Love and Forgiveness

Saying "I'm sorry" is one of the most powerful ways we parents can show our love for our troubled child. Asking forgiveness when we've been wrong is what repentance, reconciliation, and redemption are all about. Although this idea may sound strange to parents in pain, the decision to forgive our children is an important step in the process of gaining back our lives.

Parents in pain aren't the only ones who have discovered the power of healing in forgiveness. So vital is the act of asking forgiveness that it's step 8 ("Made a list of all persons we had harmed and became willing to make amends to them all") of AA's 12-step program.

In her book *Ready? Set? Go!: How Parents of Prodigals Can Get On with Their Lives,* Judy Hampton devotes an entire chapter to forgiveness. She is very straightforward: "Without forgiveness, our wounds will simply never heal. Sure, it's easier to nurture the pain. But if we want our wounds to start healing we must forgive. Forgiveness is an act of our will."[1]

Forgiveness is on us. No one can make us forgive, and it's often not easy to make ourselves forgive. But Judy Hampton is one of many voices saying that complete healing can't and won't happen if we still harbor bitter unforgiveness.

For me to move on from unforgiveness—which will help me

choose to stop enabling my son and to set healthy boundaries—I've found it necessary to look at these five areas of forgiveness:

1. Forgiving Those Who Have Hurt Us
2. Forgiving Our Adult Child
3. Forgiving Ourselves
4. Asking Forgiveness from God
5. Asking Forgiveness from Our Adult Child

Forgiving Those Who Have Hurt Us

In *Seven Prayers That Will Change Your Life Forever*, Stormie Omartian talks about a prayer of release. She begins by sharing her painful past as the often-abused daughter of a mentally ill mother. It's easy to see how her mother's behavior left Stormie with deep emotional pain and feelings of futility, hopelessness, and helplessness. Struggling for years with issues that frequently had their roots in this polluted soil of her childhood, Stormie spent decades looking for love in all the wrong places, filling the empty places in her heart and soul with empty promises and pursuits. How well I could relate! Confessing her sins to Jesus, recognizing that He had died so she could be forgiven, and naming Him her Lord entirely changed her life, but it wasn't until Stormie could forgive her mother that real healing began:

> "You don't have to *feel* forgiveness in order to say you forgive someone," [Stormie's Christian counselor] explained. "Forgiveness is something you do out of obedience to the Lord because He has forgiven *you*. You have to be willing to say, 'God, I confess hatred for my mother, and I ask Your forgiveness. I forgive her for everything she did to me. I forgive her for not loving me, and I release her into Your hands.'"[2]

Stormie goes on to talk about the power of forgiveness and the pain of unforgiveness. As children of God, we know we are forgiven when we repent. Yet the process of becoming all that God intends us to be isn't achieved with that one prayer when we recognized Jesus as our Savior. Forgiveness is a process.

Like Stormie, many of us have hurts from our past, and we need to forgive the people who have hurt us. We also need to confess any unconfessed and any unacknowledged sin of our own. The Spirit will reveal our sin when we ask Him to, and after He does, we need to ask forgiveness of the people we have hurt whether intentionally or not. Only then can we experience the freedom that God wants us to know—freedom from the bondage of guilt, blame, shame, and a host of other emotions that have undoubtedly played out in our lives in countless ways over the years.

Stormie also addresses a common thought that may be lurking in your mind—"Forgiveness doesn't make the other person right, it makes you free."[3] You might want to read that sentence again. Our forgiving others makes us free, and that's one important reason why Jesus, the apostle Paul, and preachers today call us to "forgive those who have trespassed against us." Like all of God's commands, He gives them for our good. He loves us and, in this case, wants us to know freedom from a hardened, unforgiving heart. And I can imagine what you're thinking.

"I get what you're saying, Allison, but I dealt with all that stuff years ago. I don't want to dredge it all up again. Been there; done that."

Amen! Praise God if you've already visited the places in your heart and soul that needed repair. Praise God if you have forgiven the people who hurt you, asked forgiveness of all those whom you hurt or offended, and even forgiven yourself. Let me assure you: There is no need to relive the sins of our past over and over again. Once forgiven, always forgiven—that is the power of God's love for us.

But stay with me for a minute.

Forgiving Our Adult Child

Looking at forgiveness of our adult child in conjunction with our enabling him/her—and how our forgiveness relates to healing—is a decidedly different perspective on forgiving, one that requires a new thought process and skill set.

First of all, when it comes to forgiving our adult children, we have two very specific issues going on simultaneously.

On one hand, many of us are angry at our adult children—and, in many cases, rightfully so. We may also harbor more than a little resentment and righteous indignation over how they have treated us. Many of our adult children have lied to us, stolen from us, disrespected, used, and abused us. They've forgotten or ignored our birthdays and most major holidays. They've caused us significant money problems, and we have lost respect in our community and sometimes even in our church. Many of our marriages have suffered greatly, and sometimes the family strife contributes to a divorce. Our relationships with friends and family have been neglected. Some of our adult children have used us as pawns in their game of illegal activity. We don't trust them, we can't believe them, and many of us don't even know them anymore, so far off the deep end have they gone.

Add to all this the anger we feel about what they are doing with their lives. The pain is red hot as we watch the loss of potential, the wasted life, and the opportunities they had to change but never did.

The list of what has caused us heartbreak and made us angry goes on and on.

And as we begin to distance ourselves emotionally from the situation and begin to look more objectively at the reality of what has happened, we are filled with mixed emotions—most of them negative—directed squarely at the adult child who has made such poor choices.

We must forgive them for what they have done to us even if they don't ask us for forgiveness. God's Word says, "Forgive, and you will be forgiven" (Luke 6:37). Yes, God commands us to forgive because it's good for us: We will be forgiven. Something else happens at the same time. Stormie Omartian puts it this way: "When we forgive people who have hurt us, we restore their God-given worth and value—not because they deserve it but because God has already done the same for us."[4]

Knowing in our heads that forgiveness of our prodigal is commanded and right and good for us doesn't make extending forgiveness any easier. Judy Hampton is brutally honest: "Does the very thought of making things right with your prodigal adult child make you angry?...I understand. When someone has taken your heart out and stomped on it, it's difficult to imagine you need to forgive."[5]

So, we go back to the truth that God's command—in this case, to forgive others—is for our good. That command may seem backward and impossible. Shouldn't the adult child who has turned your life upside down and, yes, stomped on your heart ask *you* for forgiveness? Yes, that request would be appropriate, but we can't wait for that to happen before we free ourselves from the chains of unforgiveness.

As for the impossible aspect of this act: When God commands us to do something, He will enable us—by the power of His Spirit—to do that thing.

Forgive your son or daughter…and free yourself.

Forgiving Ourselves

Our anger at our adult children makes forgiving them difficult. Simultaneously, so does the guilt we feel over the part we played in this drama.

Now, guilt is a good thing. Without guilt we would have no inner barometer telling us we may have done wrong, we may have made a mistake. We need to *feel*—we need to *know*—that we have done wrong, but we can't wallow in guilt, shame, and blame. We can't allow our guilt to color everything in our life with huge brushstrokes of gray, to cover truth with a murky film, or to keep us distanced from God, who wants us to know freedom from guilt as well as from anger.

During the years when I wandered lost in the desert of unbelief, I made more than a few bad choices. Some I knew were wrong as I did them. Others I justified as acceptable because the culture had preached tolerance, and I bought its lies. So I did things like live with more than one boyfriend before we were married (of course, that meant premarital sex), and I even had more than one abortion. Also, I often felt as though I coined the term "serial monogamy" because I had several live-in fiancés over the years, justifying the cohabitation because, after all, we were eventually going to be married. But somehow, we never were. My lifestyle was one of partying, drugs, alcohol, and the "if it feels good, do it" mentality so prevalent in the seventies and eighties.

I raised my son in a less-than-ideal environment, yet I felt strongly that I was being a good mother because I loved him so much, and I worked hard to keep a roof over his head and give him the things I never had as a child. I know now that I lived a selfish and sin-filled life, yet at the time I justified a great many of my lifestyle choices as the right ones.

When I look back now, it's hard to believe I'm talking about myself. Today there is little doubt in my mind that God had a plan for my life even when I didn't acknowledge His existence.

Asking Forgiveness from God

If there's a downside to making a U-turn toward God as an adult, it's the initial period of intense pain we go through when we become convicted of our sin. Because I was unfamiliar with God's truth as written in His Word, I truly had no idea how sin-filled a life I had been living. The more I read the Bible and the more I understood sin, salvation, redemption, and restoration, the more I cried out to God to forgive me. I had so much to be forgiven for.

Back in my very early days as a new Christian, I clung to a Bible verse that assured me I was on a new course in my life: "If anyone is in Christ, he is a new creation. The old has passed away; behold, the new has come" (2 Corinthians 5:17 ESV).

Countless Scripture verses guided me on my new journey, filling me with hope, healing me, and taking away my guilt and shame over the choices I had made. Understanding true repentance and forgiveness of sin was difficult for me. Remember, I had lots of layers to peel back.

We ask God to forgive our sin, cleanse our hearts, and make us new. We say, "I'm sorry, God, for all the wrong I've done. Please change my heart and give me new direction for my life." Receiving God's forgiveness initially is accepting in our heart and soul the reality of what He has done for us. He let His only Son die on the cross for your sins and mine. Although we are new creations at that point, we still possess a sin nature, so we still sin, and we still need to ask God to forgive our sins.

But we keep a short list of sins to confess. We must keep moving forward and not live in the past.

Asking Forgiveness from Our Adult Child

I know what you're thinking: *Why should I ask my child to forgive me? Shouldn't it be the other way around?* Listen to author Jill Rigby, who has a great deal of experience working with parents in pain:

> I've found that parents who refuse to accept their responsibility for the mess their kids are in can't receive healing and can't help their children heal…Accepting responsibility is always the beginning of restoration. Accepting God's forgiveness for our misguided parenting and then looking an adult child in the eye and asking for their forgiveness is powerful.[6]

This crucial step of asking your adult child to forgive you is a tough assignment, but it may be exactly what brings not only some healing to your adult child, but a growth spurt as well. Then again, asking for your adult child's forgiveness could be like pouring lighter fluid on an open flame. We won't know until we try.

In *Boundaries*, Drs. Cloud and Townsend have devoted a section to forgiveness and reconciliation. Key to their discussion is the truth that forgiveness does not always mean reconciliation. In the chapter called "Resistance to Boundaries," they say something pivotal to gaining SANITY:

> The Bible is clear about two principles: (1) We always need to forgive, but (2) we don't always achieve reconciliation. Forgiveness is something that we do in our hearts; we release someone from a debt that they owe us. We write off the person's debt, and they no longer owe us. We no longer condemn them. He is clean. Only one party is needed for forgiveness: me. The person who owes me a debt does not have to ask my forgiveness. It is a work of grace in my heart.
>
> This brings us to the second principle: we do not always receive reconciliation. God forgave the world, but the whole world is not reconciled to him. Although he may have forgiven all people, all people have not owned their

sin and appropriated forgiveness. That would be reconciliation. Forgiveness takes one; reconciliation takes two.[7]

Did you catch that? Our simply telling our adult child that he is
forgiven does not mean reconciliation will occur. He may not even be
ready to acknowledge, much less admit, that he's done anything wrong,
anything requiring our forgiveness. And even if the words "I'm sorry"
come out of his mouth, they don't necessarily indicate genuine repentance. We need to see a change in the direction of our adult child's life—
and it's possible that he will resist.

So let me caution you: Don't let your apology and request for forgiveness turn into a full-blown argument. That means not dredging
up all or even some of his past behaviors. You don't want to blame him
for anything, no matter how much at fault he may have been. At this
juncture, finger-pointing will serve no purpose.

The fact is, you are the parent, and you've made some poor enabling
choices, and now that is going to stop. However, first you need to set
things right with God and your adult child. Consider memorizing
what you'd like to say, reading it, or writing it in a letter. Often in situations like this, verbal communication may be all but impossible.
Maybe this sample request for forgiveness will be helpful:

> I need to say something to you, and this isn't easy for me
> to say. I know we've had our share of arguments over the
> years, and I've said some pretty harsh things to you. I'm
> sorry for that. I've been frustrated for a long time. Noth-
> ing I do seems to help. When things do change, it doesn't
> take long until we're right back where we started. It's like
> we're on a merry-go-round that never stops.
>
> I've been blaming you for a lot of the anger and pain I feel,
> but how I choose to feel is not your fault. My choices are my
> responsibility, just as your choices are your responsibility.
>
> Over the years, I've made some poor parenting choices. I
> want to apologize for that. I realize that every time I chose
> to accept responsibility for your actions and your choices,

I robbed you of valuable life lessons, stunted your growth as an adult, and helped make you overly dependent on me. I am truly sorry.

I also want you to know that I've learned some things that I believe will help us get off the merry-go-round, things I'd like to talk to you about soon. I know some of the changes I'm going to begin implementing are going to be difficult for you to understand at first. It may seem to you that I don't care or that I've abandoned you. But neither is true. I want you to know that I love you, and I believe in you. I also want what is best for both of us. We both deserve lives of peace, joy, happiness, and success.

Please know that I never want to cause you harm or pain. I pray that you will begin to make positive choices and fully accept the consequences of your actions and that, in doing so, you will reach a level of self-respect that will empower you to be all that God created you to be. As I said, I love you, and I believe in you. I pray that you will come to believe in yourself.

Again, I'm sorry for any damage I've done, and I'm asking you to forgive me for any pain I have caused you.

Saying words like these to your adult child won't be easy, but you must do it. You are beginning the redemptive work that will pave the way for true healing to begin.

Of course, we parents always want to respond to our children with compassion and love. For many of us, that has been all but impossible for quite some time. Our anger, animosity, and frustration run deep.

But maybe—just maybe—a season of change is now upon us.

EFFECTIVE STRATEGY

Christian forgiveness does *not* mean we ignore wrongdoings or diminish the serious nature of certain actions and behaviors. Christian forgiveness means we address negative behavior as Christ would do—head-on—and as the Bible teaches—with love and grace. Write out your plan for changes needed, and pray about the conversation you will be having with your adult child.

Chapter 13

Tough Decisions for Healthy Transformation

We parents of troubled adult children have been in a vicious cycle for years. We rescue, protect, and fix, then bring our troubled children home to heal. But it's only a matter of time before their attitude, choices, behavior, or lifestyle once again push us to our breaking point. Then, after a heated argument or altercation, they either pack up and storm off in a huff, or we feel forced to throw them out even though it breaks our heart. Once they're out of the house, we start picking up the pieces of our own broken lives, while many of them begin yet another downward spiral of self-destruction.

Once again, they're out on their own doing whatever it takes to survive, struggling to fit in, trying to make ends meet, and doing their best to navigate the health care, criminal justice, or government assistance systems and programs on their own. They're in and out of jobs, relationships, or jail. Living with friends, sleeping on someone's sofa, or shacking up with a new love interest. Sometimes taking their meds, sometimes not. Sometimes we hear from them, often we don't, and the disconnect makes us grow increasingly fearful. It isn't long, however, before some kind of drama, chaos, or crisis sends us back into the rescue, protect, and fix-it mode once more. Suddenly, our struggling adult child is back home, and the vicious cycle begins again.

Of course, we pray things will be different this time, but the only difference is that all the players are older…but not necessarily wiser. The problems our kids are struggling with appear worse—as does the growing spirit of hopelessness they can't seem to shake. This isn't how life is supposed to be.

How do we break the cycle?

While many of our choices have been well intentioned, they haven't always yielded the best results. The reality is, we've been struggling to take care of our own lives and responsibilities while rushing to the aid of our children during times of crisis, and the effort has taken a toll on us, on other family members, and, in many cases, on the very people we want to help.

We've tried to be attentive spouses or single parents, to care for other young and vulnerable children still at home, perhaps to care for our parents, and maybe even our grandchildren as well, all the while doing our best to keep our jobs, pay our bills, and address our own issues. We live that dulled existence I talked about earlier—truly living only between crises. We carry an enormous weight of responsibility for everyone and everything. Are we trying to juggle it all as penance for parenting mistakes we made in the past?

This is no way to live.

Many of our struggling adult children don't want to be a burden. They really want to make it on their own independently, and in many cases they can do exactly that—with the right structure, meds, counseling, and a treatment team working together to help them achieve their goals.

But for the most part, our troubled kids have not had that kind of helpful structure. Sadly, much of the involvement we've had with them is seen by everyone as our reacting emotionally rather than acting rationally. And in defense of my fellow parents, I assure you that this reaction is completely understandable.

Over the years, we parents of troubled children have faced one emergency after another. We have handled urgent health, housing, and financial issues. In circumstances like those, we don't have the option of strategically planning a short-term and structuring a long-term solution for the health and welfare of our adult children. We have to put out fires—yet we never fully comprehend what we could do to keep them from starting in the first place.

We want things to change. We want to make a positive difference in our adult children's lives—and improve our own as well. We want to help them get off the gerbil wheel of insanity just as much as we want to get off it ourselves.

So how do we do that? How do we take back our own lives and pour hope into theirs?

How do we stop rescuing and instead start restoring our kids?

Critical Questions

We start by answering several critical questions:

1. Are you prepared to make decisions while acting intentionally and rationally rather than reacting haphazardly and emotionally?

2. What does making a difference in the life of your troubled adult child look like to you? What does it look like to him or her?

3. Are you prepared to make an honest assessment of how ready, willing, and able you are to set new boundaries, take healthy control, and implement effective strategies to connect with your troubled adult child in helpful— not harmful—ways?

4. Are you prepared to reframe your thinking and change how you respond to your child and their problems?

5. Are you ready, willing, and able to initiate difficult conversations with your adult child in order to open healthy lines of communication and promote growth and healing for both of you?

6. What level of parental support and care are you ready, willing, and able to provide to your son or daughter over the long term?

7. Are you ready, willing, and able to develop and implement a written agreement with clearly defined rules, guidelines, and consequences for your adult child who is currently living at home or who may return home in the future?

8. How committed are you to start taking care of yourself, to rediscover God's purpose for your life, and to walk in His wisdom and Word? Are you ready to take a fresh look at who you are apart from being a parent to your troubled child?

Intentional Choices

Perhaps you're reading this book because you're ready to try a different approach to interacting with your child. Or maybe someone gave this book to you because she cares about what you're going through. What matters more than how this book got into your hands is that yours are the hands of a parent who is tired, fed up, frustrated, and afraid. You love your troubled son or daughter, but you've had enough. You just can't do this anymore. At least not the way you have been.

I understand. Completely.

As I write this, my 45-year-old son is once again in jail. I've lost track of how many times this is. His pretrial hearing is in a few weeks. On that day, the district attorney will offer x-number of years instead of going to trial, and Chris will confer with his public defender to decide whether or not to take the offer. He's looking at anywhere from 10 to 25 years.

My heart aches for him.

As part of their protocol, the jail has taken him off all his medications—including his extensive psych meds—until the jail's psychiatrist can see him. It's already been several weeks. My son is a classic example of someone with a dual diagnosis and diminished capacity after his years of substance abuse and his increasing mental illness. On disability with limited income, he rationalizes the poor choices as what he needs to do to survive—choices that act like dominoes as they fall over onto one another and bury him. Again.

I won't be flying out to attend this upcoming hearing, and after he is sentenced and moved to prison, I'm not sure how long it will be until I can visit him.

The last time he was arrested, he spent 11 months in jail before his trial. He refused to plead guilty to a crime he insisted he didn't commit. He also refused the 15-year "deal" the district attorney offered. If he went to trial and was found guilty, the minimum sentence was 25 years. I was sitting in the courtroom when the jury returned from deliberations, and the judge read, "Not guilty."

"Thank You, Jesus," I whispered as I tried to hold back the tears.

I prayed that would be the last time in a series of last times.

Alas, that wasn't to be. And as we enter another challenging season in our relationship, my prayer isn't that God will release Chris from jail, but that He will use this experience to do something transformative in Chris's heart and in his life. I pray that God will keep my son safe and fill him with a spirit of hope.

And I'm praying for myself too. I'm asking God to give me the wisdom and discernment to respond to my son and to the situation and circumstances in ways that will bring glory and honor to Him and spiritual growth to me as I walk in rational obedience instead of emotional disobedience.

While that all sounds very lofty, trust me, I'm not all that lofty. What I am is a brokenhearted mom who's "been there and done that" so many times that I now know the only way out of the pain is to push through it. I also have faith that God has a plan for my son and for me.

He has a plan for you, too, and for your troubled child.

Fellow parents, when we have critical decisions to make concerning our adult children, our first line of defense is the *S* step in SANITY. We need to STOP reacting emotionally. STOP running to the rescue. STOP doing what we always do when we think our troubled child needs us. Instead, we need to pray for wisdom from God and discernment as to what He is calling us to do.

It's time for us to make intentional choices based on information that we rationally think about and process. It's time to break the habit—prompted by our emotions—of jumping into the fray. It's good to feel things deeply. It's even better, though, when we can balance those feelings with thoughtful wisdom and discernment.

Purposeful Preparation

We are going to look at making critical decisions from a healthy place of possibility, not from fear, guilt, or obligation. We are going to consider how to approach strategically the challenges of being the parent of a troubled adult child.

So are you ready to be empowering instead of enabling? Do you want to make an impact without being interfering? I know some of these topics will be hard to read. I also know that parents like us who care deeply can stop on a dime and turn around when confronted by hard truth and convicted by the Holy Spirit. I know this...because that's what happened to me. As we proceed, keep your journal nearby and write down whatever you feel the Lord is revealing to you, saying to you, or calling you to explore further.

And remember to rely on the six steps to SANITY. They can prepare us as we make critical decisions that really can make a difference in the lives of our troubled adult children.

Critical Decisions to Make

- The Making-a-Difference Decision
- The Ready, Willing, and Able Decision
- The Where-to-Live Decision
- The Health Care Decision
- The Mental Health Provider (MHP) Decision
- The Level of Support and Care Decision

The Making-a-Difference Decision

Most parents want to make a difference in their child's life. However, that positive impact doesn't look the same for everyone, and that's okay. It's important to know what you are—and are not—ready, willing, and able to do concerning the support, recovery, and ongoing care of your troubled adult child.

To be a positive influence, we must educate ourselves about our children's illnesses—just as we would do with any other medical issue—and, whenever possible, encourage them to do the same at whatever level of comprehension they are capable.

But learning how to connect with our troubled adult children in a way that can make a difference isn't only about understanding their mental health issues or substance abuse disorders. It isn't only about knowing the associated conditions a dual diagnosis brings or being able to separate the external symptoms from the internal illnesses. Such knowledge is valuable, but there is a far more critical aspect of connecting with our struggling kids.

What making a difference is really all about is discerning the ongoing role God is calling us to have in their lives and obeying that call with love, grace, and wisdom. That approach is infinitely better than interacting with our child out of fear, guilt, or obligation. When we are following God's lead and walking in His power, our children begin to feel God's transformative love through us.

Spiritual Growth

Many of our troubled children have dug themselves into some pretty deep holes, and their only hope of climbing out is if someone extends a hand to help pull them up.

Some parents might argue this is what they've been doing for years. And they'll say that they threw out a lifeline again and again only to have it tossed back in their face. While that very well may be true, let's look at this situation from a different perspective.

Perhaps, fellow parent, the heart of the matter is not us rescuing our children and pulling them out of the pit of trial and tribulation time and again.

Perhaps the heart of the matter is really what happens to them—and us—while they're in the pit.

Is our involvement helping our children to push through the pain and learn the powerful life lessons God wants to teach them—or are we preventing that growth? Is our involvement helping to produce the strength and courage our children need to make better choices the next time they face pain, fear, or adversity—or are we getting in the way?

We also need to consider why we are caring for our adult children's needs. Do you provide what you think they need because you are afraid of the consequences if you don't? Are you acting willingly from a heart of love, or reluctantly from a sense of duty or obligation? Our ability to pour Christian hope and healing into the lives and hearts of our children is intimately connected to our spiritual obedience and growth.

Are we helping our sons and daughters gain deeper knowledge about God's ways (His kingdom) and how those ways apply to our issues in life (His righteousness)? Does the character of Christ flow through our words and deeds? Do we practice the faith that we preach?

We must ask if our involvement in our children's lives is really making a difference.

If not, what must we change?

The Ready, Willing, and Able Decision

Being ready and willing doesn't necessarily mean we are able. Jesus said in Matthew 26:41, "The spirit is willing, but the flesh is weak."

How many times have you willingly rushed in to help your adult child with a problem that at first glance appeared relatively easy to handle, yet as things began to unfold, you discovered far more layers than you imagined, many of which were beyond your ability to manage?

That was the sad situation for Suzie, a sweet woman I met years ago. She volunteered to help a local ministry update its contact management database. It was a big project, one the director of the organization had kept putting off. She was ecstatic when Suzie offered to handle it.

There was only one problem. Although Suzie was ready and willing to do the work, she was far from able—a fact the director didn't establish beforehand.

"I assumed she was computer literate and understood the software program we used," the director said. "She was so enthusiastic and seemed so capable…"

Sadly, that was not at all the case, and over the course of two weeks, sweet Suzie managed to delete over 10,000 donor names and corrupt a database with so many incorrect keystrokes and commands that it had to be scrapped entirely. The moral of the story? It's okay to be ready and willing but not able. Or able but not ready and willing. Before you commit to something, know what you are ready, willing, and able to do—or not do.

Overly helpful parents (that is, chronic enablers) tend to tackle more than we are ready, willing, and/or able to handle.

As you parent your troubled child, be aware of how ready, willing, and able you are to make critical decisions and commitments in areas that affect your health and safety, as well as the health and safety of your struggling child, and perhaps even your grandchildren. Let's vow to be intentional about looking at our level of commitment in all areas of our lives before we say yes to something else.

With each decision we make, may we clearly see the pros and the cons, the possibilities and the purpose.

Wise decisions are made when we discern the will of God, and God reveals His will to those willing to do His will. May we always be ready and willing to do what God calls us to do, knowing that He will enable us to do it.

Able Versus Capable

While the line between able and capable may seem thin, there is a distinction. For example, someone may have the ability to recognize and identify numbers, yet not be capable of understanding those numbers in the context of algebra or trigonometry. Or maybe someone is able to read the labels on five different bottles of medication and know what each is for, but not be capable of managing a complex dosing schedule on a daily basis. Some parents are able to provide shelter for a troubled adult child, but are not capable of covering the cost of health care, medications, transportation, and so on. Some of our children are able to manage self-care, complete daily chores, and even hold a job when they are living in a structured environment, but because of brain chemistry damaged by years of drug abuse, they are not capable of making those same daily choices and decisions on their own.

We need to decide what we ourselves are able and capable of doing, even as we determine what our troubled children are both able and capable of doing.

The Where-to-Live Decision

The ability to live in a place you can call your own—whether it is rented, leased, or owned—is an important part of the great American Dream. For most adults, being able to live independently is an achievable goal. However, for a person with mental illness or in substance abuse recovery, independent living often seems an unattainable dream, often because of finances.

While some of our troubled adult children can pursue an education and secure gainful employment in their given field of expertise, that path appears to be more the exception than the rule. For the vast majority, finding and keeping a job is challenging, and even then the income versus expense ratio is not favorable. For troubled adults unable to work, applying for government-assisted programs is a daunting and very lengthy process. Then, if they are accepted, the financial realities can be hard for them to comprehend.

In 2016, a person relying solely on SSI (Supplemental Security Income) received $9,156 annually—which is about 22% below the federal poverty line of $11,770 for a one-person household.[1] Furthermore, in 2016, the national average rent for a studio apartment was $752—which is 99% of the average $763 monthly SSI payment.[2] It doesn't take a mathematician to run those numbers and see a glaring problem.

As many parents well know, their adult children's struggle to find affordable housing is real. As a result, too many face inappropriate options or even homelessness. When struggling adults can't afford housing, they end up living on the streets; in homeless shelters, hospitals, jails, or overcrowded boardinghouses; or with relatives. Any of these hardly ideal living situations is a significant barrier on the journey to recovery, and living with relatives can strain even the best of relationships. Those adult children who do find and can pay for housing then often struggle every day to afford treatment and medications, let alone food, utilities, and other necessities.

One of the most challenging and most critical decisions we parents must make is whether to permit our troubled adult child to live with us, whether short term or long term. At any given time, having a troubled son or daughter living under our roof can be a blessing, a curse, or a combination of the two. If we are to make a difference in their future, we have to take a different view of how we help in this critical area—and if we allow them to move in, I can't overemphasize the need for a written and signed—by them as well as us—Residential Agreement contract that outlines household rules and expectations.

Without a doubt, finding safe and affordable housing is a significant issue in the lives of our offspring. Because this where-to-live decision is so complex, I've devoted all of chapter 15 solely to this topic, and I have included in Appendix A a template for a contract you can use.

The Health Care Decision

If you have a health problem, you go to a medical professional who specializes in treating that problem. If you have high cholesterol or are at risk of a heart attack, you see a cardiologist. If you have digestive problems, you see a gastroenterologist.

But if you face a mental health and/or substance abuse problem, where do you go first? Are you even able to prioritize your medical issues? What symptom—in an ever-increasing palette of concerns—do you address first? If you have a substance abuse disorder, mental illness, or a dual diagnosis, how do you balance information from multiple health care providers, multiple diagnoses, numerous medications, and all the associated responsibilities and consequences of this life puzzle?

And what if you don't have health care coverage and can't afford to see a primary care doctor, let alone a psychiatrist, psychologist, counselor, or therapist? What then?

Can our struggling children even get the health care they need?

Yes, but it won't be easy. And they may need our help to navigate an incredibly confusing and often convoluted system.

Helping a Troubled Adult Child to Navigate the System

Navigating the labyrinth of providers and state agencies can be challenging for someone with healthy brain chemistry. For many troubled adult children, getting through that maze can be virtually impossible, and that is often one reason they don't get the help they need.

Affordable and available health care in America—particularly mental health care and substance abuse treatment—has been a topic of discord for many years. Applying for financial aid, disability, or supplemental assistance requires a person to figure out a complicated system involving local communities, the federal government, research institutions, private companies, and other pieces that together create an intricate mosaic.

Because there are so many pieces in this puzzle, many parents feel called to lend their support in this critical area. Pray long and hard about this, ask your child if she wants your help, and be prepared to spend a great deal of time talking on the phone, acquiring the right forms, completing scads of paperwork, and jumping through more hoops than a circus dog. Prepare to be frustrated, overwhelmed, and at times outraged as you run down one rabbit trail after another only to find you received false information or filled out the wrong form.

But rest assured that if God is calling you to this task and you enter it with open eyes and an open heart, your decision can have life-changing results for your child. Being able to help our sons and daughters to get health care coverage, see a professional for an accurate diagnosis and prognosis, get the medicine they need, and perhaps arrange financial aid or SSI disability can make a profound difference in their lives.

The Mental Health Provider (MHP) Decision

Many types of mental health providers (MHP) can help our troubled children reach their recovery goals. These professionals work in inpatient facilities, such as general hospitals and psychiatric facilities, as well as outpatient facilities, such as community mental health clinics and private practices.

The job titles and specialties of these health care professionals can vary by state. Finding the right professional is easier when you understand the different areas of expertise and training.

Detailed descriptions for the professionals listed below can be found on the National Alliance on Mental Illness (NAMI) website. NAMI is one of the most comprehensive organizations serving both the patient and the advocate. Additionally, the NAMI HelpLine can assist you in finding various mental health professionals and resources in your area.

Assessment and Therapy

- Psychologists
- Counselors, Clinicians, Therapists
- Clinical Social Workers

Prescribe and Monitor Medication

- Psychiatrists
- Psychiatric or Mental Health Nurse Practitioners
- Primary Care Physicians
- Family Nurse Practitioners

Other Professionals

- Certified Peer Specialists
- Social Workers
- Pastoral Counselors

The Level of Support and Care Decision

When someone struggles with emotional or mental illness and/or substance abuse, that struggle affects every aspect of their life and everyone in their family. In most families, someone typically emerges as the primary go-to person, the one who steps up and steps in to meet the challenges of providing care and support for the loved one. In many instances, this person will face countless critical decisions, sometimes on a daily basis.

People with emotional and mental illnesses and chemically altered brains are not "crazy"; they are sick and trying to manage life despite very real health conditions that result in a wide range of incredibly complex symptoms. And, of course, those individuals also dealing with a substance abuse disorder—a dual diagnosis—have an even harder time managing life.

Some adults with these conditions are high functioning and able to live a full life with only minimal assistance. Others have a seriously diminished quality of life and struggle every day to survive. The consistently poor choices these people have made are beginning to catch up with them and, as a result, with us parents as well. These adults depend heavily on their go-to person.

Dawn is a committed parent who, like many of us, learned the hard way how to help her son. She learned that caregivers of adults with mental illness or substance abuse problems have a great amount of responsibility but very limited authority. After her son was hospitalized, Dawn faced a maze of social support services, mental health care providers, and treatment options that required competencies in social work, psychiatry, psychology, case management, negotiation, and conflict resolution.

Understandably, she was overwhelmed.

As her son's primary caregiver, she needed to learn a lot on the fly including these items:

- What is HIPPA? What could she do to overcome this obstacle so that she could be informed about her adult son's condition and participate in treatment decisions?

- What does she need in order to apply for disability and to access Medicare and Medicaid benefits?

- What mental health services are in their community, and how could her son access them?

- What are supported housing, day programs, peer support, job training, and rehabilitation—and what role would each play in her son's recovery?

- What is cognitive behavioral therapy, and how would she apply its principles?

- Nine different medications required learning about psychiatric pharmacology and drug interactions.

Mental illness often doesn't reveal itself until after a child turns 18. After that point, though, parents do not have the legal authority to force their troubled adult children to get the help they need. That's one reason why many of us have watched our children struggle, decompensate, and become statistics in a broken health care system or in the criminal justice system.

Today, the needs of our troubled adult children who are dealing with serious issues can be mind-boggling and extensive. Past or current substance abuse disorders, emotional and mental illness, and/or traumatic life experiences have completely altered the children we once knew.

As our troubled children get older, it becomes even more important that we reframe our thinking and begin to take an intentional look at how much assistance our child is going to need in the long term—and what level of care we are ready, willing, able, and capable to provide. Or not.

We parents of troubled adult children need to know how emotionally and mentally incapacitated our children are. To what degree has substance abuse affected their thinking, problem-solving, and coping mechanisms? How long have they been spiraling downward? Do they have additional physical disabilities that require an additional level of care? And what does their mental health provider (MHP) say is the prognosis?

The decision about how ready, willing, and able we are to address our children's growing needs must be made with purposeful prayer and rational thinking.

Before we parents make this critical decision, it's also important for us to honestly assess the degree to which our children are taking personal ownership of their issues. Are they willing to do whatever it takes to change their circumstances, or do they live with a noncompliant and angry spirit, blaming others for their lot in life? Will our children be receptive to new plans we want to implement, or defiant and perhaps even dangerous? Do they understand right from wrong, or is their thinking corrupt?

This list of what-ifs and "do they or don't they?" could go on for pages.

Clearly, we do not have access to a one-size-fits-all method for knowing how any person will respond to change, and for our troubled children, the prospects can range from appreciative to abhorrent, from favorable to frightful.

This uncertainty is often why many parents fear ever rocking the boat. Why we stay on the dizzying gerbil wheel of insanity year after year, repeating our same behaviors, yet expecting different results.

The time for change has come.

EFFECTIVE STRATEGY

We have covered a lot of ground in this chapter. Now I want you to retrace your steps. Review each of the six "Critical Decisions to Make" and determine where you and/or your troubled child are regarding that particular decision. Pray about the decisions you feel God is calling you to make, and write them down. Doing so will ground you in the rational, think-it-through approach to the parenting challenges you face.

Chapter 14

Healthy Support and
Compassionate Communication

ow we face perhaps an even harder question. How ready, willing, and able do we think our troubled adult children are
for the road ahead? Are they cooperative, prepared to seek
help, and committed to making different choices? Or are our children
completely noncompliant? We must consider their attitude about the
future and how ready they are for a change before we commit our time
and our energy, our finances and our futures to their well-being.

As you contemplate and pray about these critical decisions, it will
be important to sit down and calmly communicate with your son or
daughter about the choices you feel God is calling you to make. But
our children must be willing to talk to us. We can't force them.

And our struggling sons and daughters need to be heard without
our trying to fix them. In order for us to have a chance to listen to their
heart with nonjudgmental love and compassion, they must trust that
they can talk to us.

In many cases, there is a wide chasm separating us from compassionate communication with our troubled adult child. In many cases, it
may take time to rebuild trust; we can't force our children to accept our
help, and we don't want to try. This entire exercise in intentional decisions is about us learning to connect with our adult children in a new
way. To make this easier, I've included a few letters in Appendix B at the

end of the book that might help you express your thoughts and feelings. There are also numerous letters and resources available on my website at www.AllisonBottke.com. You might read one of them aloud to your child, or give it to them to process in their own time. You will know what is best if you pray for wisdom and discernment and then follow the call on your heart. (If your child is in a critical place requiring legal or in-patient intervention, talk with a support person to decide the best way to communicate this decision to your child. Be prepared for all scenarios, and approach this situation with caution and prayer.)

In His Word, Jesus prompts us to come to Him when we need help and guidance:

> Ask and it will be given to you; seek and you will find; knock and the door will be opened to you. For everyone who asks receives; the one who seeks finds; and to the one who knocks, the door will be opened. Which of you, if his son asks for bread, will give him a stone? Or if he asks for a fish, will give him a snake? If you, then, though you are evil, know how to give good gifts to your children, how much more will your Father in heaven give good gifts to those who ask Him! (Matthew 7:7-11).

If you aren't sure about what course of action to take, wait. Don't rush God. He has promised to give you good gifts. In this case, the good gifts of wisdom, insight, and hope.

Where Is God Calling You?

Supporting our troubled children isn't an all-or-nothing prospect. Think of it as an a la carte menu. Some of our kids may need help figuring out how to develop a medication dosage system that works for them, while others may find this aspect of self-care easy to manage. Some may need help completing a lengthy health care assistance form, and others may just need you to review their completed form to make sure they did everything right. And just as our children have varying degrees of needs, we have varying degrees of what we are ready, willing, and able to do for them.

Obviously, full-time, in-home caregiving is not possible for every parent, but not every troubled child will need such high-level care. Take a minute to think about what your troubled adult child actually needs. Write in your notebook an honest assessment of what you see as your child's short- and long-term needs.

Parents, we can definitely assist and empower our troubled adult children as they work to build a strong treatment team that will facilitate a healthy, productive, and hopeful life. It's safe to say that most of our struggling children already have at least the beginning of a support system that includes health care professionals, perhaps a counselor, therapist, psychiatrist, pharmacist, social worker, parole officer, and maybe even a dietitian or physical therapist.

Clearly, you and I don't need to be our child's all or nothing. Our involvement in our child's life is about what role God is calling us to have in this season of life and how ready, willing, and able we are to step up, step back, or step out of the picture. And to do either of the latter two without guilt.

Levels of Support

What exactly are some levels of support we can provide our adult children? Knowing the degree of responsibility and commitment at each level will help you better determine what role God is calling you to play in your child's life. The following information is general; it is not intended to serve as legal advice. Also, pray for wisdom and discernment. Ask God to give you a clear sense of what He is calling you to do regarding your child. And remember that He will never call you to do more than you are able to do. Never.

That said, also remember that you can't do it all, and you don't have to.

So set healthy, godly boundaries. Be able to say no with firmness and love and, yes, with authenticity. Don't wait until you have been stretched to your limit to say no. That kind of no is often the result of frustration, anger, and simply being burned out—and that kind of no is hard to speak with love. Also understand that there's nothing authentic about saying yes out of guilt, fear, or obligation.

Let me offer you this reassurance as well: We can begin to connect with our troubled adult children in ways that can make a difference when we make intentional choices and critical decisions from a heart of love.

So, where is God calling you? What level of support does He want you to provide for your adult child?

- Supportive Parent (as opposed to enabler/rescuer)

- Patient Advocate (medium level of responsibility)

- Treatment Guardianship (high level of responsibility)

- Conservatorship (high level of responsibility)

- Setting Them Free and Letting Them Go (very little active support or involvement; usually reserved for noncompliant or ASPD [antisocial personality disorder] adult children)

Supportive Parent

First of all, a supportive parent is very different from an enabling, interfering, suffocating, controlling, angry, or ambivalent parent.

As supportive parents, we agree to offer an ear to listen and a shoulder to cry on, and, if asked by our adult children, we will give our best counsel regarding decisions they face.

While an incredibly valuable role, this level of "quiet" power is most likely unfamiliar to many rescuer/fix-it parents. After all, our pattern of well-intentioned interference and unsolicited advice has been our standard operating procedure for so long that we don't even see its downside.

In instances where trust must be rebuilt, you might say to your child, "I want to help, but I know in the past I may have been following more my own agenda than yours, and I'm sorry. I need to trust you to make the decisions you feel are best for your life, and I'd like to help you on that journey. Could we talk about ways I might be helpful?"

In this role, you might agree to drive your son to one AA meeting a week or pay for childcare for your daughter's baby—your grandchild—two nights a week so she can go to school. Grab your notebook and begin to write down ways you can be supportive. Be careful not to overdo it; we don't want to enable. And try not to have all your support be financial, even though this might be your child's biggest need.

Additionally, this level of being a supportive parent takes on new meaning if your troubled child is living with you now or will be coming to live with you soon.

Patient Advocate

A supportive parent times ten, a patient advocate is the glue that holds the treatment team together. Emotional or mental illness—that may or may not be combined with a dual diagnosis of substance abuse—causes stress for patients and their families. Our children's judgment is impaired. Our kids are not at their best when they are sick, but which one of us is?

Many troubled adult children need someone who can look out for their best interests and help them navigate a confusing health care system. They need, in other words, an advocate—a supporter, believer, sponsor, promoter, campaigner, backer, and/or spokesperson all rolled into one. As advocates for our children, we have full access to their health care records and treatment team directives. This level of involvement does not authorize us to make any decisions about requesting, accepting, or refusing treatment. But we do speak on behalf of our adult child in acquiring and sharing health care information. Clearly, our role as an advocate requires the complete trust of our child.

An effective advocate is able to work well with other members of the health care team, such as doctors and nurses. An advocate may be a spouse, a child, a different relative, or a close friend. Another type of advocate is a professional advocate: Hospitals usually have professionals called patient representatives or patient advocates, but social workers, nurses, and chaplains may also fill this role. These advocates can often be very helpful in cutting through red tape. I encourage you to find out if your hospital has professional advocates available and, if so, how they may be able to help you.

Guardianship, Treatment Guardianship, and/or Conservatorship

Guardianship, treatment guardianship, and conservatorship are legal designations used in the court cases that arrange for a person (called a guardian or a conservator)—or sometimes a company or other entity (called a conservator)—to make certain decisions for another person (the ward). A guardianship deals with nonfinancial decisions, while a conservatorship deals with financial decisions. A guardianship or conservatorship can be set up for people whose decision-making capacity is so impaired that they are unable to keep themselves safe or to provide for their daily necessities. The person must be at risk of physical injury or illness.

The Slippery Slope of Setting Up a Guardianship or Conservatorship

In our country, when we become adults, we are generally able to make decisions for ourselves. We can even make decisions that others think are wrong. Because our freedom to make decisions for ourselves is such a basic right, it can only be taken away from us for a very good reason. And even then, the court must consider the "least restrictive alternative"; the court must take away the smallest amount of decision making possible. Guardianship or conservatorship is only needed if the person's decision making threatens his or her welfare. Neither option should be used simply because the person has a certain disability or diagnosis or because he or she makes a decision that other people do not understand or agree with.

At the next level of support is the treatment guardian, a person appointed by a court to make mental health treatment decisions on behalf of individuals whom the court finds—by "clear and convincing" evidence—incapable of making their own treatment decisions or providing informed consent.

What is informed consent? A physician must provide information about recommended treatment. A person who uses this information and, after considering the risks and benefits of the proposed treatment, decides to accept or reject treatment is practicing informed consent or making an informed decision. Our adult children are assumed capable of giving or withholding informed consent. If, however, we come to believe our children are not capable of informed consent, we may file a petition for a treatment guardian. This court appointment can last no longer than one year; at that point, the process must be conducted again.

When possible, we should consult not only our troubled adult children about the support options they have, but their health professionals, attorneys, friends, and other family members as well. Then we will be better prepared to make decisions that will be best for our children. In the event of a noncompliant patient—if the treatment guardian believes the patient has not followed the treatment and the decisions the guardian has made—the guardian can apply for an enforcement order that authorizes the patient to be taken to an evaluation facility. The choice to pursue an enforcement order must be made only after careful study of what an enforcement order entails and full consideration of the ramifications of the decision.

An adult guardianship case may involve both guardians and conservators, and this arrangement allows the handling of medical appointments, medical decisions, and living arrangements. Conservatorship is adult guardianship that includes assistance in managing personal and financial affairs, such as checking and savings accounts, investments, and the sale of real estate, for instance.

The Legal Levels of Support

I want to assure you that, if necessary, we parents can obtain certain levels of legal authority through the court system, should life-threatening issues need immediate intervention. Before taking a step of this magnitude, do your research and carefully, prayerfully consider the consequences of every decision you need to make. The most critical decisions we may ever make on behalf of our troubled children are those that take away their rights. Search your heart for your motivation and goal. Meet with a support team. Pray for wisdom and discernment.

Jane James, executive director of the Stark County branch of the National Alliance on Mental Illness, adds this point: "An absolute last resort for intervention is for a parent to attempt to obtain guardianship of his or her child, which would allow the parent to control the child's medical care. But…it could cause more problems because it takes away a person's authority and can lead to confrontation."[1]

In this instance, I encourage you to apply the *A* step in SANITY and ASSEMBLE supportive people, particularly other parents who have taken legal steps to help their children. Conduct thorough research and seek legal counsel if you are considering a more prominent role—a higher level of support and greater responsibility—in the life of your adult child.

Do Your Homework and Consider the Consequences

In the event you choose a level of support that gives you legal rights to make decisions for your adult child, be aware of the additional emotional, financial, and time commitment. In some cases, these commitments will be long term. Learn all you can about these commitments beforehand. You don't want any surprises on down the line. Also, the more prepared you are for best- *and* worst-case scenarios, the better. Getting professional financial and legal advice is critical, and you can find resources through federal, state, and local governments as well.

Sadly, what many of us will learn when we seek help is…the quality and quantity of help that could assist our children is all about the money. We may encounter a lack of community resources and a shortage of affordable mental health care providers. A person can wait weeks, even months, to get an appointment that may or may not be helpful. Without a long-term solution for meeting the needs of an adult child with mental illness or a dual diagnosis, we caregivers too often watch our loved one get caught—year after year—in the cycle of repeated hospitalizations, criminalization, and substance abuse.

This gerbil wheel of insanity is what I've experienced with my son for decades.

After years of navigating through the laborious systems and procedures of government-funded programs and services, including hospitals and clinics in three different states, I've come to a great many conclusions. Yet the primary lesson I want to share with you now is that for anyone facing emotional or mental illness or dual diagnosis substance abuse components, it is imperative to have a trustworthy and calm person acting as a patient advocate and keeping track of everything and everyone associated with the patient's care. Think of this person like the construction supervisor on a major shopping center development where multiple stores—all with different logistical needs—are being built simultaneously. At any given time, sometimes at a moment's notice, someone must be aware of how, when, why, and who is involved in connecting all the pieces.

If God is calling you to advocate on behalf of your son or daughter, it will be a tremendous responsibility. But maybe you won't be the advocate, and that's okay too. I encourage you to empower your troubled child to find someone—with or without your help.

You're Not Alone

Every day we parents of troubled adult children wait for another crisis, another emergency call, another drama that will turn our lives upside down. For many of us, the endless stress and uncertainty lead to our own depression and anxiety. Sometimes, we lose our jobs, our income, even our marriages.

And as that unfolds around us, we are watching our sons and daughters get lost in a rabbit hole.

It's heartbreaking.

> *My daughter is 45 and has suffered from bipolar with psychosis since the age of 19. After years of self-medicating substance abuse, she was recently given a dual-diagnosis. I am her parent-caregiver, and she lives with me. At one point she was stable for ten years, but finding that stabilizing balance now seems impossible. I wish I had someone to talk with who understands what we go through as parent-caregivers.*

> *My son was diagnosed with bipolar at age 18. Now 32, he has been in assisted living or dual diagnosis treatment centers from one end of the state to the other. Self-medication became his way to cope with his illness. He would get himself kicked out*

of a program so he could return home, but we finally had to tell him he could not live at home. We were no longer going to accept him and his friends destroying our property and stealing our belongings.

My son's story is one of increasing symptoms of mental illness and more than 15 years of substance abuse. My biggest challenge now is trying to figure out how to make accommodations for him after I am gone.

Our son was diagnosed with schizophrenia at age 19. Now 24, he has had many horrible life experiences due to his mental illness. He lost his job, car, apartment, friends, and girlfriend. Felony charges were later dismissed, and his more than 16 hospitalizations were mostly involuntary. We had to make the soul-wrenching decision to say our son could not return to our home. Despite this, he is doing much better now with the right combination of meds that control his symptoms, a group home he resides in (only a few blocks from our house!), and some insight into his illness now that has resulted in more med compliance and far fewer hospitalizations.

Our Financial Commitment

We must consider how ready, willing, and able we are to make a long-term financial commitment to our children's care before we make it. What that care entails and its cost will be different for each of us. Also, some of us may still be in our earning years, but others may be near retirement or already there. We must also consider the possible or even probable financial commitment of caring for our grandkids. And if we choose to cover or at least assist with the financial costs of rehab or the institutionalization of our troubled adult child—long or short term—we must be prepared for that cost. Consulting a financial adviser and/or attorney would be wise.

Compassionate Commitment

Let's face it. Life with our troubled adult kids is going to get more and more complicated. Realistically, how much time and energy are you ready, willing, and able to share? You're not being selfish; you are taking an open-eyed look at reality. If you are still working full time, for instance, how and when will you find the time to care for your child?

If your spirit is willing, but your flesh is simply unable to accomplish what needs to be done, it is absolutely okay to look for other alternatives. Perhaps you can share the responsibilities.

It's better for us to be honest and authentic than to overcommit and let our children down.

EFFECTIVE STRATEGY

What level of support do you feel called to provide? Use your notebook to record your thoughts, questions, concerns, and prayers.

- Remember that your caregiving isn't to be an obligation you reluctantly take on. May it instead be a choice you freely make.

- Know that if God is calling you to care for your child in this season, He will equip you with what you need. In fact, armed with His wisdom and His Word and approaching your child with a spirit of love and grace, you may be able to provide your son or daughter with a new lease on life.

- Resist the urge to act quickly. Instead, think thoroughly and prayerfully about the situation.

Chapter 15

When Your Troubled Adult Child Lives with You

When you open your door to an emotionally troubled off-spring, be sure you open your heart as well. That heart where Christ dwells and from which God's love flows through you and out into the world.

Sadly, in many instances, this selfless act of hope and sacrifice is met with anger, blame, and vehement denial of any culpability, with accusations and lies that leave us bruised, battered, heartbroken, and wondering where we went wrong. Why are we so quick to blame ourselves? And why do we keep repeating the same behavior, expecting different results?

The fact is, where our children live is a difficult topic for us parents of troubled adult children. I know this because of the sheer volume of email I get from desperate dads and manic moms.

First, some musing. I'm not sure how or when it happened, but something has shifted in our culture. A great many parents today seem to have lost confidence in their ability and even their right to exercise healthy parental control and influence. Fearful of defining healthy boundaries and of holding their offspring accountable when those boundaries are violated, these passive parents question just about everything they say and do. Their passivity contributes to growing unrest in the household, and it does little to build spiritual and structural integrity in the parent/child relationship.

Let me ask you, how effective would a treatment program be if the people for whom it was developed were put in charge? Picture what could happen if patients were in control of a critical care facility, if mentally ill individuals were in control of the psychiatric hospital, if convicted inmates were in control of the prison, or if uneducated children were in control of the school curriculum.

These hypothetical scenarios are as absurd as they are inconceivable—and no one who needs help is helped. Yet this is what we parents are doing every time we allow our troubled adult children into our home without providing structured guidelines and clearly defined consequences for violating those guidelines. In essence, we place our troubled son or daughter in control of our household.

Parents, it's time for you to control the narrative!

The following is a letter from a couple who lost complete control in their home. Their cries for help and advice leave me shaking my head in disbelief...

Dear Allison,

We are done! My husband and I are tired of fighting with our 26-year-old daughter. We have been trying forever to get her to move out of our home. She is disrespectful, uses foul language, and screams at both of us regularly. We will never forget the vile things she has said to us. What happened to our sweet girl?

She has become a criminal (shoplifting and drug abuse) and has even stolen from us. She won't work, yet always has money for cigarettes and takeout. She refuses to help around the house and never cleans her room. She has various men coming in and out of our home at all hours. God knows what they are doing. Probably buying drugs. If it weren't for our beautiful grandson who also lives here, we would have sent her packing long ago. But what can we do about this?

We feel like prisoners in our own home. We are afraid to leave the house in case something terrible happens. We haven't told her this yet, but since we can't get her to live on her own, we are planning to sell the house and finally do some traveling.

Any advice you can give would be so helpful.

Sincerely,
Fed Up in Arizona

Let me assure you, this letter is not a fabrication.

It's also not an isolated incident. In countless homes across the country where parents have provided refuge and respite for a troubled adult child, these parents have become prisoners to the choices their children are making. Many of these parents feel the only way to break free is to move.

Who considers selling their home to get the peace they have worked hard for all their adult life? I have to wonder, what else will these parents surrender to their noncompliant troubled adult child? Their health? Marriage? Faith? Freedom? Perhaps their sanity?

Here's my advice to Fed Up in Arizona. First, set aside the question, "What happened to our sweet girl?" and instead ask yourself, "What happened to us? How did we get to this place where we are allowing our daughter to disrespect, manipulate, and control us?"

The mother wrote, "She has various men coming in and out of our home at all hours. God knows what they are doing. Probably buying drugs." To which I must ask, "Why are you allowing this? It's your home. Put a stop to it now."

Then she said with resignation, "But when all is said and done, what can we really do about this?" To that, I say, "A lot! You can do a lot!"

Parents, I'm not going to sugarcoat the severity of situations like this one. We parents have got to take healthy and godly control of the narrative; we need to step up and parent in a way that helps our kids rather than further handicaps them.

When you allow your children to return home during a difficult season, your influence can be negative or positive; your sharing life under the same roof can encourage new spiritual growth or stifle it.

Which one will it be?

Seasons of Change

There are challenging seasons in life when adult children find themselves in transition, and their returning home for a brief season can be a very good option. Their parents are happy to help because they know the situation truly is only temporary. In fact, many parents look forward to having offspring under their roof once again, particularly when the adult child has exhibited a sense of responsibility, the parent/child relationship is healthy, and, as a result, these children have grown up secure, confident, compassionate, honest, and wise.

Consider, too, those troubled adult children who are anything but responsible, their relationship with their parents is strained, and those parents know only too well what the experience will be like if they allow these children to return home. These adult children can be insecure, indecisive, fearful, manipulative, disrespectful, and sometimes even dangerous. You want to help, but you don't know how much of your child's drama, chaos, and crisis you can take again. You feel powerless and uncertain about how to comfort and help them, and you have this gnawing sense that maybe you aren't really helping them by frequently coming to their rescue. But, like Fed Up in Arizona, you think, *What can I do?*

With all due respect—and as I told Fed Up—you can do a great deal.

Moving in with parents can be a life-saving opportunity for a troubled adult child. It can be a chance to get back on their feet. For caring parents to be in a position to offer much-needed respite to troubled adult children can be a blessing, especially if they have been living on the streets or out of their car; sleeping on someone's sofa or in a homeless shelter; or being evicted from their apartment or home. Maybe these adult children are escaping a toxic relationship, or the negative influences of their old circle of friends and need to make a complete break. Or maybe they're trying to stay clean and sober. Finally, if they're getting out of jail or prison, or if they're nearing the end of an extended stay in a residential inpatient treatment center or hospital, having somewhere safe to go can make the transition to "the outside" easier.

Whatever their circumstances, we love our kids and worry about them, especially when they are struggling or in pain. Our natural instinct is to step in and stop that pain.

However—and this is where it gets challenging—for some kids, the season of struggling appears never ending, and we sense it's beginning to take a toll on us physically and emotionally, not to mention financially. Furthermore, no matter what we as parents say or do, many of our kids continue making the same poor choices. We wonder, *Is it ever okay to say, "No, you can't come home"?* Is it okay to step away from our adult children and allow them the opportunity to deal with their trials and tribulations? Or are we being insensitive to their pain and selfish about our wishes? And what if our grandchildren are involved? Who is responsible for them? These questions are not easy to answer.

We sigh, and we wonder, *When will our adult children learn? Why don't they change?* It seems to us that the only thing changing is the ever-increasing severity of the consequences of their poor choices.

Whether your troubled adult child is currently living with you or you are considering allowing them to return, I have some tools you can use if you don't want this vicious cycle of insanity to continue into perpetuity. Basically, you must address not only the reasons for their inability to maintain an independent lifestyle but what part you have played in perpetuating the revolving front door.

Also, the better questions to ask ourselves are, *When will we learn?* and *Why don't we change?*

The most challenging reason adult children return home is because they are in serious trouble. Although many of these kids have had good intentions, the choices they made were anything but good. In the majority of these cases, the added component of past or present substance abuse disorders and/or emotional or mental illness has added levels of complexity that have often rendered them incapable of making healthy decisions.

As we move forward in this chapter, our primary focus will be on this category of adult children. These struggling offspring return home because:

- They lost a job, got divorced, had a baby out of wedlock, or were blindsided by a toxic relationship. They have no money, no health insurance, and no hope.

- They have a substance abuse disorder and/or mental illness that threatens their ability to care for themselves and has left them overwhelmed.

- They have been incarcerated and have nowhere else to go upon release.

- They have become homeless due to substance abuse, untreated mental illness, and/or refusal to take prescribed medication.

- They have alienated everyone close to them and exhausted all other resources. If we don't welcome them, they will be living on the streets or end up back in prison.

In any of the above instances, your troubled adult child may also have custody of one or more children—your grandchildren—and, yes, this adds yet another layer of complexity to the already complex circumstances. These situations frequently cause high levels of stress, fear, anger, and emotional fragility for the troubled adult child and, yes, for you as well.

Troubled adult children who return home bring with them a host of problems, and all too often—because parents haven't changed how they respond to those problems—it's only a matter of time before some drama, chaos, or crisis makes the situation untenable for everyone.

The cycle of insanity continues…

Help! I'm Almost Homeless

When our troubled adult children find themselves in a state of possible homelessness and ask (beg) us for help, our first instincts are to allow them to come home. In many cases, we already know (or suspect) their skills of living an independent life are challenged either by mental illness or addiction. So—and particularly when innocent grandchildren are involved—we feel obligated to help. We're afraid for their safety and just can't imagine how they will survive out in the world if we don't take them in. At the same time, we're also afraid of what will happen once they are living with us again.

Sounds like a no-win situation…We know how difficult it is for our adult children to reintegrate into society, especially when they have a criminal record, or when they refuse or consistently forget to take their prescribed medications. Yet, we also remember how disrespectful and outright aggressive these children have been with us in the past and how effectively they manipulate us so that we can't tell the difference between their truth and their lies. Furthermore, some of us have other family members at home to protect from the behaviors we have seen in the past from this child.

Nonetheless, we feel obligated to say yes when they ask to live with us and don't seem to have any other options.

In many cases, their return home comes on the heels of an emergency—when emotions are high, time is of the essence, and decisions must be made quickly. In these cases, we typically don't have a plan in place or any idea of a time line for moving out—if moving out will even be possible. Suddenly, you're living in limbo—praying that you won't regret your decision, but knowing in your heart you most likely will. It's only a matter of time…as the parents below can attest:

> *My son is 31 and expresses his anger on me regularly. I am planning to tell him he has to go to an anger management class or move out of my home. The only reason I haven't yet is because of my four-year-old grandchild.*

> *I am a serial enabler battling to move forward with a 24-year-old son who has massive fear-of-failure and self-esteem issues. A particular dilemma is responding to his tantrums.*

> *I have a son who is very manipulative and verbally abusive. He needs help! He and my five-year-old grandchild moved in with me six months ago. His violent behavior is escalating, and it is not healthy for me or his daughter to be around him! The only reason I didn't kick him out of my home last week was that I think he would hurt himself. On the other hand, it isn't safe to be around him at all, so I don't want him in my home even one more day. I am tired of giving him time and money and being verbally abused, but I don't want him to hurt himself.*

Whether or not we admit it or they realize it, the troubled children who come in and out of our homes need more than a roof over their head. They need to find a way to climb out of the deep hole their distorted thinking and poor choices have landed them in. They also need faith, hope, and lots of love and compassion—and that's a tall order when their negative behavior often makes them hard to like, much less love.

Truthfully, a great many of our troubled adult children need a high level of accountability and care. Quite frankly, most of their parents—most of us—are not able to provide that. Understanding our limitations is critical when we once again open our door to our troubled children. We do them and ourselves a disservice when we don't apply the *I* step in SANITY and IMPLEMENT a clearly defined plan of action.

Remember, I am not talking about your typical American adult child (if there is such a thing anymore); I am talking about people we moms and dads sometimes don't even recognize. People who have substance-related and addictive disorders, accompanied by an emotional or mental illness like bipolar and related disorders, depressive disorders, anxiety disorders, panic attacks, PTSD, personality disorders, and a host of other emotional and mental health illnesses. Issues that have a profound effect on an adult child's behavior and—if we aren't very careful—on our behavior as well. How will we respond?

Break the Cycle

Many of our troubled adult children will struggle for the rest of their lives. But that doesn't mean their struggle must become yours. These pages offer steps you can take and effective strategies you can implement if you're willing to do the work.

We parents of troubled adult children must learn how to hold ourselves accountable for our actions and, when possible, hold our adult children accountable for theirs. We must learn *how* and *when* to say no with firmness and love and how to say yes with honest authenticity. Most important, we must learn how to respond to our situations and circumstances in godly ways that strengthen rather than tear apart the fragile fabric of our relationships with our troubled kids.

May we also keep in mind that change is the only constant in life. Whether we embrace it or fight against it is our choice. I believe that many of us have been approaching change the wrong way. We need to be wise in identifying what we can change and then intentional and strategic about how we make that change happen.

Probably many things need to change in the lives of our troubled adult children, but our responsibility is not to lay out what they are or dictate why and how they need to change. In fact, unless we have taken over legal guardianship or conservatorship of our child's life, we do not even have that power.

So, when your adult child comes to live with you, you will undoubtedly want to implement changes, but the only thing you can actually control is expectations concerning household rules and how you are going to respond to what may be a never-ending series of trials and tribulations in your child's life.

The Strength of Structure

One of the most critical components of any successful residential treatment program is the much-needed structure it provides residents. In addition to outlining what will be expected from the participant, the structure is also necessary for the health and safety of everyone living in the facility. Can you imagine what it would be like if men and women struggling with substance abuse disorders, emotional and mental illness, dual diagnosis, and a wide range of personal issues had absolutely no structure or guidelines for how to live? What would it be like for them to live in a place where no defined rules, regulations, responsibilities, or consequences exist? In essence, the patients would be in charge—and how helpful would that treatment center be?

If you're sitting there shaking your head and thinking, *Allison, that's insane*, I have to agree.

Which brings me to a very important question I need to ask you.

Reality Check

If you think the idea of patients being in charge of their own care is insane, then why—when you know your troubled adult child struggles with substance abuse issues and/or has a history of emotional or mental illness—do you allow him to come back home and live without providing a clearly defined structure? When your child has consistently demonstrated an inability to make wise choices, why on earth would you welcome her home without putting in writing what you are providing and what you expect from her as long as she is living under your roof? And what about that duration? How long will she be in your home? Have you discussed this topic with your son or daughter and established a time frame? Is their occupancy temporary or permanent, short term or long term?

And, most important, what are your adult child's goals for this season of growth? And what are yours? Do you have a plan to help your child outline a path forward?

Before we move on, I need to reinforce the importance of putting in writing the parameters of your child's stay. Are you once again opening your door based on yet another verbal agreement that is subject not only to interpretation but to recollection as well? A recollection that might be impaired? Remember, brain-related issues like substance abuse and mental illness affect an individual's ability to comprehend and remember. Put the agreement in writing and get it signed before your troubled child goes to bed that first night.

Parents, we also need to be mindful when we open our doors that our kids have demonstrated behaviors that range from disconcerting to dangerous. They may be seriously impulsive or become frustrated easily; some are paranoid, and others, psychotic. Some troubled adult children will use negative behavior to frighten, manipulate, and control family members. In many cases, they are living with an impaired reality, but a psychiatric disorder like that is an *explanation* for behavior, *not an excuse*.

Furthermore, many of our kids have abused drugs, committed crimes, and participated in one antisocial activity after another, and some are intimately familiar with the criminal justice system. These kids have experienced many life transitions. They have been between jobs, between relationships, between jail sentences, between stints in rehab, and sadly, sometimes hovering between life and death.

These kids are like natural disasters, threatening to disrupt your life with a never-ending series of storms, tornadoes, and hurricanes. The extent of the devastation they leave in their wake threatens your emotional, spiritual, physical, and financial health. So why, I must ask, don't you prepare yourself?

Disaster Preparedness

In 1979, President Jimmy Carter signed the executive order that created the Federal Emergency Management Agency (FEMA). Committed to protecting and serving the American people, FEMA coordinates the federal government's efforts to prepare for, prevent, mitigate the effects of, respond to, and recover from all domestic disasters, whether natural or man-made, including acts of terror.[1] FEMA's vision is "A Nation Prepared."

As parents who live precariously between the crisis situations in the lives of our troubled adult children, we have much to learn from FEMA's strategy. Simply put, we must become prepared parents!

Yet, when we fear for our children, something happens in our hearts and minds that seems to obliterate common sense. All memory of lessons learned from past experiences—lessons learned the hard way—seems to vanish.

What keeps us from holding our adult children accountable for their actions—many of which are sinful? The Bible tells us that if we do not confront people to take ownership of their problems, we share in the guilt of those problems.[2] The prophet Ezekiel quoted the Lord on a related topic: "If I announce that someone evil is going to die but you do not warn him to change his ways so that he can save his life, he will die, still a sinner, but I will hold you responsible for his death. If you do warn an evil man and he doesn't stop sinning, he will die, still a sinner, but your life will be spared" (3:18-19 GNT). Scripture is very straightforward in its presentation of this critical spiritual growth/real-life issue. Again, if we don't confront people to take ownership of their problems, we share in the guilt of those problems.

Ex Post Facto

Without a doubt, the return of a troubled adult child into our home can be uncomfortable in many ways. The most uncomfortable may be establishing healthy boundaries. That conversation, though, can also be an opportunity for you to speak hope and healing into your child. Know that the clear rules, expectations, and consequences you have established are the hallmark of a healthy connection.

Whether our adult child is responsible or irresponsible, our choosing to say yes when a child asks to return home should always come with a written plan that not only protects you but gives your adult child a clear picture of expectations and responsibilities. Two well-meaning parents learned this lesson the hard way.

Happily retired, Susan and George had just moved into their new home in a different state when their eldest son called. He was in an outpatient drug rehabilitation program, and the desperation in his voice was palpable. "I'm trying to stay clean, but I just can't do it here. There's too much temptation, too many bad memories. Can I come home for a little while to get myself back on track?"

"This wasn't the first time he asked to come home, and none of the past experiences had turned out well. But we wanted to believe him, to give him a chance, so we said yes, and we verbally outlined what we expected," George said.

Parents, I have to ask, why do you think *this time* things will be different?

Is there some concrete proof that your troubled adult child has had a spiritual epiphany or a significant change of heart? Most likely not, so in a few months, you'll be regretting your decision and moving quickly toward a breaking point.

For Susan and George, their son's old manipulative behaviors slipped back into the picture, and their internal red flags began to wave. Not wanting life to spiral out of control (again), they started to second-guess themselves: *Perhaps he isn't using again...Maybe he really did attend the NA meeting and forgot to get his card signed...Maybe we need to give him the benefit of the doubt and just trust him.*

Folks, more trust and freedom isn't what troubled kids need when they are spiraling out of control—and taking you with them.

Often, what these kids desperately need is more structure.

And when we lovingly explain that structure and clearly show our children how it encourages growth and measures success, structure can be a life changer. For your adult child—and for you.

Parents, please remember, our kids are dealing with bipolar disorder, depression, paranoid schizophrenia, psychosis, substance abuse disorders, and often dual diagnosis with a substance abuse disorder and a mental health issue combined. These kids are fragile and frustrated. Depressed and suicidal. Disrespectful and emotionally volatile. Physically and verbally abusive. Some take, forget, or refuse medication for their diagnosed mental health problems. Others self-medicate with illegal drugs and deny that anything is psychologically wrong.

Sadly, many of these troubled children are so damaged and distraught they have little ability to function rationally for day-to-day decisions, let alone make wise and strategic decisions for their future that is, at best, precarious.

Why, then, do we climb onto the vicious gerbil wheel of insanity by continually treating our troubled kids as if they are "emotionally healthy" kids?

What is wrong with us?

Let's make that wrong right...

Ex post facto is Latin for "a thing done afterward." In this context that "thing" is a structure for our children. It is never too late to develop a written agreement, even if your adult child is already living with you and has been for a while. This is your home, and you have every right to develop and present them with a written plan of action.

Stop being a victim. You control the narrative. Take healthy control in and of your own home.

Escalation Leading to Eviction

So you reach your breaking point and find yourself shouting, "Get out! Enough is enough!"

This is when, in a best-case scenario, your child leaves in a huff and moves in with a friend or another relative, most likely someone they have brainwashed into thinking that you are completely unreasonable and heartless. In a worst-case scenario, this point is when life can get frightfully dark and sometimes dangerous. And that's why we parents hesitate to bring up these issues that might trigger our children's rage or hatred or worse.

That frightful darkness and danger can play out as overdoses, suicide attempts, psychotic breaks, criminal behavior, and other seriously poor choices. Choices that force our hand and give us no other option but to evict our children from our home, have them committed to a psychiatric facility, obtain a restraining warrant order of protection, call the police, call child protective services (CPS), or apply for legal guardianship so we can intervene and supervise the care of our troubled adult child.

In circumstances like these, parents beat themselves up for agreeing to this living situation, especially if this experience has happened before. Maybe more than once. Should you find yourself in that position, take the *S* step in SANITY and STOP beating yourself up! This habitual action of self-blame by parents who really do care and want so much to help their kids has absolutely zero positive impact on the situation.

So let's look at how to improve our connection with our troubled kids. After all, we want to actually be of some assistance to them.

Parents, Wake Up!

When it comes to your home, whose name is listed as the "responsible party" on the bank mortgage or rental agreement? Who makes the monthly payment required by those legally binding documents? Who pays the utilities on time, thus securing an uninterrupted flow of electricity, water, and gas? If you have Internet service or cable television, who pays the bill that enables Wifi connections?

I would hazard to guess that you are the responsible party. Correct?

Okay. So how many times have you said—or at least strongly implied—"If you want to live in my house, you must obey my rules"? We parents often say this, but we find it difficult to enforce rules that are verbally vague and often left to personal interpretation.

But the financial responsibilities are not the only consideration when an adult child moves back into the home. We parents also find ourselves dealing with our child's health and welfare. What can we do to help these adults realize how critical it is that they make better choices? What can we do, if anything, to encourage and empower our children to stop messing up their lives?

Quite frankly, many troubled adult children need to be in an environment—like an inpatient treatment center—that offers a lot of accountability. Many of our children need professional help and guidance—including medical attention, psychological care, and often occupational training—from a team of health care providers. Yet the cost of these programs is often prohibitive, or our children don't or can't adhere to the established rules of conduct and are expelled from the program.

In which case, they are now, once again, under our care.

And this is when critical decisions—like those discussed in the previous two chapters—must be made.

First Time or Last Time?

Carter was so excited when he moved into his own place with a couple of roommates right after graduating from high school. He planned to take a few classes at the local community college and work part-time. With three guys sharing expenses, they could make it work.

Sadly, things began to unravel less than six months into the experience when one roommate lost his job, and the other got arrested for dealing heroin. Over the next couple years, Carter tried to juggle everything on his own—work, school, expenses, a series of roommates (some great, some not so great), and a growing addiction to alcohol. His friends partied hard, and he had never realized how much he liked beer—and pot. When he had a tooth pulled, the dentist prescribed hydrocodone (an opioid), and when the prescription ran out, one of his roommates introduced him to a girl who could get more—if he wanted it. He did.

When he finally asked his parents for help, he had hit bottom for the first time in his life.

His parents welcomed him back with open arms—but not an open checkbook and not without a written plan. Before agreeing to help, his parents spent an entire weekend developing a plan of action. And how did things work out?

"It was the best thing my parents could have done for me," Carter says. "I was pretty messed up at first, and they agreed to let me move back home only if I completed a three-month inpatient addiction recovery program—and they made it clear that they would fund that program just one time. And if I didn't complete the program or got thrown out, the option to come home was off the table. They were so calm when they told me this; I didn't doubt they meant every word.

"I also had to agree to follow a written plan after I got out of the program. I was ticked off at first, but when I stopped being stupid, I realized I was being given a pretty good deal. I knew what was expected of me and how long I could stay on a short-term temporary basis. They also gave me the option to stay longer if I went back to college or to a trade school. The whole document was maxed out with information, stuff I had never even thought about, like who buys my toothpaste and shampoo and stuff—and that was me. My parents are realtors, so I guess the whole contract thing was logical to them, and it worked for me."

If this is the first time you are allowing your troubled adult child to return home, you can learn much from Carter's parents. If opening the door to your child is yet another in a long history of your doing so, it's important that you take a completely different approach. Or you could do what you've always done and once again accept your position as the vulnerable victim, in control of nothing, and living at the whim and dictates of your troubled child.

The choice is yours. You have the chance to impact your child's future by how you respond to the situation.

Interpretation

"Living on the streets was pretty intense. It lasted just four months, but it felt like four years. When my parents said I could come home, I didn't hesitate. I needed some time to rest and regroup. It was great to be able to sleep without worrying about someone stealing my stuff or fearing for my life."

While that comment from a troubled adult child is completely understandable, a certain phrase needs to be addressed: How long is "some time"? A couple weeks, a couple months, or a couple years?

Let's say you have welcomed your offspring home. You have no written agreement, but you feel confident that you understand why your child is in this current situation. You also believe that you have made yourself and your expectations clear in the verbal communication you have had. That said, grab your notebook and, based on the conversation you have had with your child, write out your answers to the following ten questions:

> (Name) was having problems with (1. what?) and got into trouble because of (2. what?). So the plan is for (name) to live at home for (3. how long?) in order to (4. do what?). And in order to accomplish #4, he/she has to (5. do what?). If he/she doesn't accomplish this goal within (6. what time frame?), (7. what will happen?). (Name) has a long-term goal to (8. do what?). In order to help (name) accomplish this goal, I have agreed to (9. do what?) for (10. how long?).

Were you able to answer all ten questions based on what you remember from your verbal discussion with your child? How similar do you think your child's answers would be if he or she filled in the blanks?

Conveying verbally all the critical information in that paragraph is never wise. Expecting your adult child to understand your expectations exactly as you meant them is almost an impossibility. We can't interact with our troubled adult children as though they have no problems.

Therefore, not having in writing your clearly defined answers to these important questions places you in a very weak position. Filling in the blanks as soon as possible and presenting them to your child in writing is the next crucial step—and you need to do so now.

I realize that much about this issue is tied up in our own mixed-up emotions, fears, and unrealistic expectations. Yes, we parents have to deal with our own stuff. And we can absolutely do so even while we are navigating a challenging season with our children *if* we honestly acknowledge and accept what our stuff is—and what our children's stuff is.

Eyes Wide Open: Zero-Tolerance Issues

As we know, many of our kids have brain-related illnesses, so they don't think the way we do. They don't think the way we think they ought to think. Furthermore, addicted or mentally ill adult children may exhibit frightening and dangerous behaviors—behaviors that can damage a home and property, threaten their parents' lives, the lives of other family members, and even their own lives.

Despite whatever illnesses our children are dealing with, we absolutely cannot allow their harmful and dangerous behavior to go unchecked. We must establish zero-tolerance boundaries clearly and immediately—boundaries that set forth specific consequences, one of which will be the immediate removal by the police if necessary.

Talk about this zero-tolerance policy rationally with your spouse or support partner so you will know what to do in case your troubled adult child does one or more of the following:

- Physically assaults anyone in your home

- Makes verbal or physical threats against you or others in the home

- Willfully damages your home or personal property

- Brings illegal drugs into your home or misuses prescription drugs

- Brings weapons or other dangerous items or substances into your home

And I am not the only one who insists on this approach. Safety is a real issue that absolutely cannot be ignored.

In *When Your Adult Child Breaks Your Heart*, Dr. Joel Young is straightforward: "When your adult child threatens you, it means that he can no longer live in your home because you are not safe. Violence perpetrated by adult children can and does happen, and no parents can be expected to live in fear."[3]

Young tells parents that we are able to seek a restraining order on our children if doing so ensures our safety and adds this: "You are not a failed parent if you take this action…Most mentally ill people are not violent but do not assume that your adult child would never harm you. Adult children have injured or even killed their parents and family while in the throes of rage, psychosis, or a reality that is impaired by drugs and alcohol."[4]

We parents of troubled adult children need to live in reality and deal wisely with its every aspect.

A Written Plan

When adult kids (troubled or not) live with us and share our resources, it is imperative that we convey—in writing—our expectations and their responsibilities. Equally important is a defined list of the consequences should our children violate the agreement. Think of this as a fair and reasonable exercise that protects everyone.

But as a parent once said to me, "This is my daughter and her baby, not some stranger. She's having a hard time financially on her own. It's only for a little while until she can save some money to get ahead. It would be insulting if I treat her like a tenant and make her sign a formal agreement."

How insulting was it to this mother when, a few days after her daughter moved in, she quit her job because she didn't like her boss always telling her what to do? And what about the unexpected drain on this mom's weekly paycheck when she had to start buying baby formula, diapers, and virtually everything her daughter and granddaughter needed because her daughter refused to find a new job or apply for government assistance? "What do I look like, a welfare bum?" her daughter said. And how insulting was it when this daughter brought home a new boyfriend she met at her Narconon meeting while her mom was at work and, before leaving, he helped himself to Mom's heirloom jewelry and her new laptop computer?

Folks, it's time to change how you view the situations and circumstances that involve adult children who are struggling with substance abuse disorders and/or mental illness.

What has to happen before you realize your child's rules of engagement have changed—and yours need to change too?

A written and signed Residential Agreement leaves no room for assumptions or wrong thinking (see Appendix A). This contract promotes a home atmosphere that is comfortable for everyone. It frees you from taking on unexpected and sometimes uncomfortable roles such as policeman, banker, babysitter, and cook, to name just a few. This agreement sets forth your child's responsibilities. Ideally, this contract gives you the freedom to focus on your relationship instead of constantly policing his or her actions. Ultimately, it protects you and your adult child.

Remember, though, that a signed agreement isn't worth the paper it's written on if the consequences aren't carried out. This is where all our good intentions come crashing down if we don't stay the course.

EFFECTIVE STRATEGY

We've probably all heard the statement, "Say what you mean and mean what you say." And we've probably all appreciated its wisdom. But living it out can be tough. So get your journal and spend a few minutes looking in the mirror of this powerful sentence.

What keeps you from saying what you mean to your troubled adult child? What practical step(s) can you take to overcome your hesitation or even fear? When will you take that first step?

Maybe sometimes your words seem spot-on, but you don't mean them. You know you won't act on them. What is that dynamic all about? What can and will you do to get past your reluctance to act on what you tell your child?

Looking at both parts of this wise statement helps us see that our getting healthier will only help our troubled adult children get healthy.

Chapter 16

Put It in Writing

There isn't any reason in the world why an adult child struggling with depression, anxiety, neurosis, or even bipolar disorder should not be given responsibilities similar to other people their age. Our not doing so can prevent their progress toward healthy independence. Remember, each and every one of us—not just those who are labeled "mentally ill" or in addiction recovery—has hurdles to overcome. All of us need to learn how to trust God and make our own way in the world despite our limitations.

Trusting God means believing in His promises, like the one in Jeremiah 29:11 that I suggested you post on your refrigerator—"'I know the plans I have for you,' declares the LORD, 'plans to prosper you and not to harm you, plans to give you hope and a future.'"

Remember that the word *prosper* is translated from the word *shalom,* a word of blessing that means peace, wholeness, and prosperity. It is God's desire for our children to one day find peace, to be whole, and to physically, spiritually, and emotionally prosper in life. He wants them restored even more than we do.

Identify Your Goals

Be absolutely honest with yourself. Is your goal to keep your adult child tethered to you in unhealthy dependence? Or do you truly want to motivate him or her toward some level of healthy independence? Hopefully, it's the latter.

However, what that level of healthy independence will look like depends on what your troubled child is actually capable of achieving. This is one reason why having a diagnosis and prognosis from a mental health professional (MHP) is critical.

Even if adult children who aren't "troubled" are living at home, they're still costing parents money. Studies show that parents provide emotional, financial, and practical help to adult kids in unprecedented numbers. Not surprisingly, most of that financial impact involves taking care of children with emotional or mental illness or struggling with addictions or substance abuse.

Many troubled adult children, however, can thrive in an environment that provides structure, such as an assisted living or group home. Others may need more managed long-term care. Whether this care happens in your home or elsewhere is one of those critical decisions we talked about earlier. You shouldn't feel guilty if you're not able to provide full-time care. There is no shame in not having the physical ability or necessary training to do so.

I have, however, heard many success stories about troubled adult children who remain in the family home and, with structure as well as the support of a treatment team, are able to work toward a level of independence never expected. Understanding what your child is capable of (through a professional diagnosis and prognosis) is critical. Being able to identify the level of support (if any) you feel God is calling you to provide with genuine love, rather than fear, guilt, or obligation, is next. Then, sitting down to discuss all of this with your son or daughter is essential at this critical stage of your adult child's life.

God's Plan

Many of our troubled children have lost years of their lives to drug abuse or undiagnosed mental illness, and they need to be the ones who seek to reclaim those years. We can't do it for them. Neither can we force them to open the eyes of their heart to see a Father who loves them and wants the best for them. But we can provide an environment that could nurture a spiritual awakening in our children.

After all, the big picture of God's plan should affect everything we do in life, not just what we do on Sundays. How we connect with Jesus every day will impact how we connect with everyone, especially our troubled adult child.

Take a minute to imagine God speaking to you right now: "How much do you want your child to know about Me?"

If your answer to God is, "Nothing is more important to me than having my child love You, walk with You, and serve You," the best thing you can do is to show your child what a heart for God looks like.

When we love and obey God, it shows in what we do, how we speak, the ways we interact with people, how we spend our time. Our love for God can show in every aspect and every moment of our lives.

Furthermore, God trains us to be who He needs us to be—and He doesn't need us to be our child's Savior. That is God's responsibility.

What God wants from us is to depend on Him: "I am the vine; you are the branches. If you remain in me and I in you, you will bear much fruit; apart from me you can do nothing" (John 15:5).

As our expert Gardener, God will prune our branches by helping us get untangled from unhealthy dependence. He will free us from trying to rescue and fix our adult children—and we can instead allow Him to rescue and fix us. Our wise and good God wants us to make authentic, heartfelt choices that enable us to experience His truth and love and to actively pursue spiritual growth in ways that affect real life.

As we walk in God's Word and will, pouring out our heartache to Him, we can find hope, healing, and direction. And we desperately need those blessings as we seek how best to connect with our troubled adult children and help them experience that pushing through their struggles makes them stronger. Our knowing and obeying God's Word is essential: "All Scripture is inspired by God and is useful for teaching the truth, rebuking error, correcting faults, and giving instruction for right living, so that the person who serves God may be fully qualified and equipped to do every kind of good deed" (2 Timothy 3:16-17 GNT). We want the Lord to enable us to love our adult children wisely and well with His love.

Your Personal Life Plan

As you undoubtedly noticed long ago, we parents wear many hats. Unfortunately, not all of us are able to wear all those hats in a healthy, balanced way. We end up pushing our own hats to the side and wearing hats our children or other family members should be wearing. Over time, we find ourselves knee-deep in hats, most of which don't even belong to us. If that's your current situation, it's time to sort out those hats!

Whether or not our troubled adult children are living with us, our ability to connect with them in a healthy way comes down to our ability to look at ourselves first. Many of us are guilty of overparenting—of doing too much for our kids and expecting too little from them.

At this stage of your parenting, you might seriously consider seeking your own professional therapy and counseling. (You won't be the first parent of a troubled child to do so!) We can benefit from the wise perspective of professionals who aren't emotionally tied to our circumstances. They can help us gain clarity and perspective. They can also be part of your living out the *A* step in SANITY: Make it a priority to ASSEMBLE a group of supportive people who can speak truth into your life and hold you accountable to living it out for your good—and your child's as well.

Helping or Handicapping?

As parents of troubled children, we often limit what we expect of them because of the "handicaps" we see in their lives, such "disadvantages" as the inability to keep a job, get a job, pay their bills, take their meds, or battle a drug habit. We limit their capabilities when we make excuses for them.

You may be thinking, *But, Allison, my child literally can't do that!*

To which I ask, "How do you know that? Are you sure?"

Perhaps you've heard the story of the butterfly that couldn't fly after a well-intentioned observer assisted its escape from its chrysalis. Rather than a beautiful butterfly, it emerged with a swollen body and shriveled wings. Science has discovered that butterflies must struggle to get out of the chrysalis in order for their wings to be strong enough to fly.

The same is true for our kids. They will gain strength as they struggle.

So rather than blaming our children's addiction, illness, or disability for all their problems, let's start cheering them over their hurdles. Mastering emotional health, spiritual growth, and real-life demands is a process. A demanding process. We parents can help our sons and daughters to negotiate this difficult path from present self to future self—or we can continue to handicap them with our well-intentioned "help" (also known as enabling). We cannot run our adult children's race for them, but that truth doesn't keep some of us from trying.

Our children will never learn to fly if we keep trying to help them every step of the way.

The Time Is Now

We've reached the point in our journey together where it's time to lay down some house rules for adult children living in our home now or who may be returning in the future.

How do we establish reasonable ground rules, manage expectations and responsibilities, and follow through with consequences? Hands down, one of the best ways to do this is to write up a contract that everyone in the home will sign and stick to.

This critical exercise will enable you to regain control in your home. In addition, the written contract will set a plumb line of behavioral expectations that can help an adult child who isn't always able to think clearly or who has never had clear guidelines by which to live.

When we are discussing and signing this agreement, we need to clarify that establishing house rules with a contract isn't an attempt to control our children's lives. Try to communicate the big difference between house rules and life rules and acknowledge that we parents can't set rules for how our adult child chooses to live. However, we can—and we should—set rules for their behavior in *our* home and consequences when those rules are broken.

Again, clarify that you're not coming up with all these rules to punish or demean your child, but to reduce and eliminate stress. Explain that your desire is to establish in the home an atmosphere of hope and healing that will promote family harmony as well as your child's success.

Also, it's important to remember that some troubled adult children have selective memory. Whether that tendency is intentional or the symptom of a legitimate brain-related disorder, our children don't always hear or remember things the same way we do. Frankly, our memory might not be so great either. Putting family rules in writing helps us back up our words and leaves little room for argument should memory fail either one of us.

Having a written Residential Agreement with clearly defined expectations, responsibilities, and house rules as well as specific consequences for any violation truly is one of the wisest actions a parent can take when an adult child lives at home or wishes to return.

How to Change a Life

Remember, you and I cannot change our adult children. We cannot help individuals who don't want to get well or who think they don't need to get well. No matter how distorted we feel their thinking is, their decision not to take prescribed medication, work with the therapist, or follow house rules is their adult decision. Unless we have been granted legal rights to make decisions on our children's behalf, how they choose to live their life is...their choice.

And that, in fact, is how God treats us: He gives us free will. Yes, it would be easier for Him to zap us and make us obey, but God doesn't do that. Free will allows us to make our own choices and then face the consequences of those choices. God's kindness is always there for us, but His wisdom and love let us go rogue anytime we choose. We must give our adult children that same freedom.

In this context, then, as we apply the *Y* step in SANITY and YIELD everything to God, we need to learn to rest in Him—in His faithfulness, sovereignty, power, grace, and love. We may not see how God is working in our children's lives, but we can trust that He is not neglecting them. We don't know when we will see the results of God's work, so we need to wait on God's timing. That waiting is one of the hardest things a parent must do when a beloved child is being ravaged by drugs, perverted by sin, or incapacitated by emotional or mental illness.

But waiting on God does not mean we sit back and do nothing. Keep reading.

When we set healthy boundaries and enforce them, we are both exhibiting self-control and taking responsibility for ourselves. Taking responsibility for someone else's anger, pouting, disappointments, addiction, or illness can damage and even destroy our relationship with that person. Instead of taking responsibility *for* the choices our troubled children make, we need to show our responsibility *to* them by confronting their wrong behavior and evil whenever we see it. This is what truly loving our child means, but living out this kind of responsible behavior is usually incredibly difficult for parents. If we don't, though, our troubled child will remain in bondage to sin, poor choices, and negative behavior.

Ultimately, freedom comes to any one of us when we are lovingly confronted about our sins and our errors. That's why the way we confront our troubled adult children is vital in forging a healthy connection with them. Sadly, previous conversations may have had the opposite effect and actually damaged our relationship.

This is where the *S* step in SANITY—the call to STOP—is incredibly valuable. Stop, regroup, and take time to think. The goal is to communicate rationally, not alienate because of our emotional outburst. And healthy, rational communication is best done when we are able to exercise self-control, especially if our child is unable to do so.

Be Smart, Stand Firm

Some of our troubled adult kids are quite brilliant negotiators and manipulators. They can talk their way out of anything. They know our buttons—and they're not afraid to push them.

These kids can also be very good at blaming everyone else for their circumstances and not taking any responsibility for why they are where they are. Their norm is a victim mentality, but we parents must stand strong. We must be ready, willing, and able to apply the six steps to SANITY and jump off the infernal gerbil wheel of insanity once and for all.

What helps me and may help you is visualizing my adult child as healthy, whole, and restored. Holding onto your vision can help keep you from being sucked into the vacuum of your child's manipulation and blame.

Your Priorities, Their Consequences

You have probably encountered one of the most challenging aspects of connecting with our adult children: Quite often they do not see as priority issues what we see as priority issues. Remember, we cannot and should not try to force them to see our way. Accepting our children as they are, respecting their choice to be that way, and then giving them appropriate consequences—or allowing the natural consequences to unfold—is a much better path for us parents to take. When we accept our adult children as they are and let them experience the consequences of their choices and behavior, we are making healthy choices.

Also healthy is having your house rules address what *you* regard as the priority issues. List those that you are most concerned about. Then prioritize the items on your list, starting with the most pressing issue.

Perhaps the most troubling issue is your child's drug addiction. Establish a house rule that no drugs, drug usage, drug paraphernalia, magazines, books, or clothing that encourages or even mentions drugs will be permitted in or around your home at any time. And the consequences of breaking that rule will be immediate eviction from the house. No warnings.

Perhaps it makes you crazy not only that your son goes out partying almost every night, but also that he is never quiet when he gets home in the wee hours of the morning. Because a good night's sleep is a priority for you, you might wish to include a curfew time in your house rules along with a specific consequence for breaking curfew.

We also need to give our adult children specific responsibilities, assign them daily and weekly household chores, require them to get a part-time job, and/or have them cook a meal for the family once a week. Some agreements will include scaling back the parents' financial support, and some will require getting a medical/professional diagnosis. If our adult children do not adhere to the house rules, they must face the consequences of their choices. We must not interfere.

If letting them experience the consequences for their choices seems impossible, keep in mind that neither your adult child, other members of your family, or you personally will live out your potential if everything at home stays the same. Change is necessary. The decisions and choices your troubled adult child is making are sucking the life out of you and everyone who loves him/her.

Be brave. Be strong. Be prepared.

A Permanent Fixture

Now for a different scenario. What if our adult child has never left the nest? Our approach will depend on the adult child's age. We will address the situation entirely differently if our adult children are in their early twenties rather than in their thirties, their forties, or maybe even their fifties.

Whatever our adult children's ages, our first step is to identify whether they are emotionally and mentally capable of living independently. They may have simply grown too comfortable being at home and have little motivation to move out. At the other extreme might be a severe emotional or mental health issue, in which case it's vital to get professional input to ascertain what level of independence (if any) we can expect.

Whether a troubled adult child lives with us out of choice or necessity, an unhealthy dependence can result if we don't address the living arrangement in therapeutic ways that encourage our child's growth and development.

If a diagnosis by a mental health professional indicates independent living is possible, design your Residential Agreement to reflect stages of independence. The first step, for instance, would be to get a job. That would be followed by such independent acts as saving a set amount of money, paying tickets to get their driver's license back, etc.

In the event the doctor's diagnosis indicates that independent living is less probable or even unlikely, we must very carefully present house rules and discuss what we feel God is calling us to do to support our seriously troubled child.

May we establish reasonable expectations for our troubled adult children, whatever the diagnosis. And may we always speak hope and healing into our children's hearts.

Consider Your Commitment

Whether it's house rules or life goals for independence, we must pray for wisdom and guidance about how to present these written documents and discernment as to when. We must ask God to enable us to speak with compassion and genuine love—and enable our child to hear our heart. If your adult child does not live at home, you can still share your thoughts about how you feel God is calling you to help, particularly if one goal is to wean them off any enabling support you've been giving them. You might, for instance, be taking away financial support if your child does not get a medical diagnosis or attend the recommended therapy groups. Or you might start saying no to free childcare when your child wants to go out partying with friends.

Let me summarize some key questions to ask yourself as you draft your house rules and before you present them to your children:

- What is your ultimate reason for developing a Residential Agreement?
- How disabled or handicapped is your adult child?
- What level of independence can your son or daughter realistically achieve?
- What is your child's official medical diagnosis?
- Are you ready, willing, and able to advocate on behalf of your adult child?
- Is your son or daughter willing to let you do so?
- What reasons and goals would motivate you to advocate for your adult child?
- What medications does your child need—and why?
  - » What are the current dosages?
  - » Are the meds self-dispensed or monitored by an advocate?

- What kind of work is or could your adult child be doing?
  » What expenses does he/she have?
  » What money management skills would help your child? Who would be best to help him learn?
- What are your child's personal goals for his/her life?
- On a scale of one to ten, how committed to change and growth do you think your child is? Support that answer with a few specifics from your child's life.

Innocent Parties

In the event we have other children—especially minors—living at home, we must look at the influence a troubled adult child might have on them. The welfare of existing members must be carefully considered before we allow a troubled adult to return home—or remain in the home. Talk to the members of your family about having the troubled person live with them. Ask them what, if anything, worries them about that possibility. Open the lines of communication. If necessary, you can add to the contract a house rule that addresses any concerns that are raised.

Or, as a result of this conversation, you may decide that having your troubled child back home is not an option at this time.

Present the House Rules and Control the Narrative

Sometimes it's virtually impossible to sit down and communicate our thoughts to our adult child in a way that's rational and unemotional. The topic of new house rules can be especially challenging. One of the best ways to communicate effectively—and, no, this option is not a cop-out—is to write down what you want to say and read it out loud to them. (See a few sample letters in Appendix B at the back of the book.)

As I've said, troubled adult children are often master manipulators of their frustrated and desperate parents. They know exactly the guilt-triggering, hurtful comments and threats to say to their emotionally exhausted parents. "Okay, great. If you aren't going to help me, I'll just end up on the street and die!" Or "Stop pressuring me to get a job, or I'll do something drastic!" And then the biggie: "What kind of cruel parent kicks their kid to the curb when he/she needs help? You don't know what love is!"

Sadly, your guilt—that, in most cases, is not justified—makes you vulnerable to the manipulations of your troubled child.

Parents, you must recognize the manipulating and stand strong.

Calculated Consequences

Trevor was waiting in the kitchen when his mother returned from work, and he wasted no time expressing his anger.

"Well, I hope you're satisfied! Look what I got today!" He waved a piece of paper as his mother calmly placed her purse on the counter. "You didn't pay the insurance, and the cop gave me a ticket. It's gonna cost hundreds."

"Why were you stopped by the police?" his mother quietly asked as she sat at the counter and waited for his answer.

"That's not the point!"

It was very much the point, but his mom had prepared for her son's outburst and didn't engage in the argument. She watched as her son tried to gauge her response—or, rather, her lack of response. In the past, she'd have already grabbed the ticket from his hand and been screaming at him about how irresponsible he is.

"It's a fix-it ticket, so when you pay it," her son continued, "I can take the receipt to the courthouse and…"

"No," she calmly said.

"No? What? You're not gonna pay it?"

"Trevor, we spoke about this months ago. I told you I would stop paying your auto insurance this month. The date is written on the financial agreement letter you signed."

Although this mom's voice was calm and steady, she was shaking inside, fearful of what might happen. But she had promised herself that this time she would not back down—and she was determined to keep that promise to herself. Very aware that the tone, the interactions, and the way things happened in her home had to change, she knew *she* had to change.

What If...?

Most parents find it relatively easy to identify the house rules, but establishing a specific and appropriate consequence for each potential violation is a much harder task. It's not like we can send our adult children to a time-out chair or ground them for a week.

Because considering as many consequences as possible is critical to effectively enforcing house rules, I want you to grab your notebook and make a list of consequences associated with the house rules you have established. *What if Susie brings home a stranger when we're at work? What if Johnny steals from us? What if Andrea comes home drunk or high? What if Brent hits one of us?*

In the scenario above, Trevor's mother had rehearsed how she would respond to her son if he got a ticket, had his car impounded, or even got arrested as a result of not paying his auto insurance. Like her, we are less likely to fold under pressure if we've considered all the possible infractions of the rules and settled on the consequences beforehand. Crucial to the effectiveness of this structure for our adult children is clarity. There must be no ambiguity in what we write down. We must clearly lay out the consequences, and we must enforce what we clearly communicate.

Of course we can't expect our children's initial response to the consequences to be pretty. Our troubled adult children will be angry, or they may go into victim mode. Trapped in their cocoon of self-pity and emotional pain, they will probably blame us. But we can be prepared. Having written down possible what-if consequences will empower us to calmly respond with wisdom and insight rather than an emotional outburst.

The level of commitment it takes for us to develop this list of what-ifs and consequences—to develop the entire document—is one reason parents simply don't draft a formal contract. So instead, they fall into doing things the way they've always been done. If that default approach describes what is happening in your home, how's that working for you?

Let's choose a different path. Let's invest time, energy, and prayer in the development of a Residential Agreement contract and the consequences of breaking each rule. Remember, though, that if you want these house rules to be taken seriously, you have no other option but to follow up on the associated consequences.

Period.

You and I will lose all credibility if we waver or get caught up in manipulative negotiations.

God gives us choices every day. He waits for you and me to make the right ones. And He's waiting for our troubled adult children to make the right decisions too. A Residential Agreement will help make that waiting time easier and healthier for both our children and ourselves.

Positive Outcomes

Like God Himself and blessed by His comforting peace, we parents are also waiting for our troubled adult children to make the right decisions—and I want to tell you there is hope. I've seen relationships restored and lives radically changed. I've read the stories. My goal in this book is to help you CONNECT with your adult child. I'm praying for you to CONNECT as a result of the positive, hope-giving outcomes of the new approach you are choosing.

In your journal, make a list of possible positive outcomes of establishing house rules and of the other forms of support you feel called to provide. These positives don't have to be all about your troubled child. You and your marriage or your other children may greatly benefit from steps you originally took with your troubled son or daughter in mind.

Here are some examples of possible positive outcomes:

- My son may begin to feel a sense of self-respect that will transfer into the way he lives.

- My marriage may take a turn for the better as we focus on taking care of ourselves.

- We may have money to repair the roof of the garage now that we aren't supporting our daughter and her husband financially.

- I may have extra money to pay for piano lessons for my younger daughter.

Negative Outcomes

Despite some very real reasons for hope, we can sometimes be overwhelmed by our thoughts about possible negative consequences our adult children might experience. Maybe one or more of these thoughts have entered your mind:

- If I send my adult child away, he may die from drugs, violence, and criminal behavior.
- Without our financial help, there's no telling what he will do to get money.
- The thought of my child living on the street, selling her body, or being in jail breaks my heart. I can't let that happen.
- My parents would help him—and disown me.

The sad truth is, all of these possibilities could indeed happen. Many negative consequences may occur as a result of the changes we are about to make—changes that will affect our adult children. Review every possible scenario imaginable to prepare yourself for their reactions and protests. You can't keep the outbursts from happening, but you can prepare yourself for the possibility.

But please don't focus too much on the possible negative consequences! Look back at the list of positive possibilities of your steps toward health. Let's not forget God's many promises that He will help us in times of trouble and—this is an amazing and wonderful truth—that God loves our child more than we do. It's hard to fathom, but it's true.

The Most Painful Consequence

If after careful consideration, prayer, and godly counsel, we decide that it's time to implement change at home, we truly have no idea how our adult children will fare.

Many will, I'm sure, discover strength and courage they didn't know they had. Some will experience great difficulty during the transition, but eventually flourish with their newfound independence and self-respect. Still others may experience significant physical and emotional pain, which will not be easy for us to see.

Every parent also has the horrific fear that their troubled adult child won't make it. This fear became reality for Steve and Lynne. They discovered that their 15-year-old son was already heavily using drugs and alcohol—and they were shocked.

They thought about their son's life: "We raised him in a wonderfully loving Christian home, where affirmation flowed daily, yet respect and discipline were taught. We could not figure out why he would choose to walk a path that was so destructive to himself and contrary to our lifestyle and beliefs." Maybe you have felt what Steve and Lynne did. We can be blindsided when we learn what our children are involved in.

The next 12 years of their son's life were an emotional roller coaster for Steve and Lynne: "He gravitated toward the dark edge, and once the drugs captured him, he was in bondage. We did our best not to enable…There were times we would hang up the phone or walk away. There is a vicious cycle when your adult child is on the brink of death. Any discouragement could make a parent's biggest fear a harsh reality, so you do your best to keep emotion and reality in balance. It got to the point, though, that when he threatened to 'end it all,' we had to release him to the Lord and walk away. We couldn't allow the instability of our beloved son to bring us financial ruin. We were already emotionally and mentally spent."

We parents of troubled adult children clearly hear the heartbreak in Steve and Lynne's story. We moms and dads feel such an overwhelming love for our children, and we have dreamed big dreams for them. When their life journeys go sideways, we pray for a miracle. We ask God to heal their brokenness, to heal their illnesses, to free them from bondage, and to send away their demons. But sometimes our child's freedom will take him or her away from us.

Tragically, a drug overdose took the life of their son when he was 27. Steve and Lynne may never have whole hearts.

Loss of life is the most painful consequence that a parent who has a troubled adult child can experience.

Such was also the case with Marjorie, a divorced mother of two. Having exhausted most of their retirement savings, Marjorie's parents refused to give her any more money to fund her gambling addiction. In their seventies and now in serious financial trouble, they didn't know how they were going to pay their own bills, and there was no way they could cover several thousand dollars of bad checks when their daughter asked yet again to be bailed out. It wasn't long before, faced with financial ruin from her gambling, Marjorie drove her car to an abandoned garage, attached one end of a garden hose to the exhaust pipe of her car, and stuck the other end through a crack in the window. Her lifeless body was discovered a week later.

When our troubled children struggle with addictions, substance abuse, or mental illness, their death is a real possibility, and so is the parents' fear of that outcome.

Every time the phone rings late at night or there is a knock on the door when I'm not expecting anyone, I fear this is the time I will have to identify my son's body at the morgue. I've relived this horrifying dream so many times that my heart is numb. And I know I'm not alone.

The world is at best an amazing place filled with opportunity and wonder—and, at worst, a dark place teeming with evil and despair. The consequences of poor choices can range from the loss of a job to the loss of a life. Whatever the loss—but especially when our child's life is lost—may God help us to realize that the negative choices our adult children made were not our fault.

It's Not Our Fault

Every action in life has consequences, and that may be a painful lesson for our kids to learn.

Remember Trevor? He eventually paid the ticket he received for driving without insurance—because he himself had missed the insurance payment. Trevor also managed to get auto insurance. It wasn't the end of the world as Trevor knew it, but it took every ounce of energy his mom had to stand firm as he dealt with the consequences of his actions. *His* actions. Not his mom's.

You need to see and believe, parents, that it's not our fault if our adult child doesn't wake up in time to get to his job and gets fired and therefore doesn't get paid and therefore can't pay his child support and thus gets arrested. It's not our fault if he doesn't have clean clothes to wear to his job interview or gas in his car to get to work. It's not our fault if his cell phone gets shut off for nonpayment, or he gets evicted for not paying his rent. It's not our fault if he fails another class because he didn't stay home to do his homework and instead went out to party. It's not our fault if he says yes to the drug pusher who hands him a dirty needle or if he gets behind the wheel of an automobile while drunk and ends up killing an innocent bystander. It's not our fault if he gets caught up in illegal activity that lands him behind bars, and it's not our fault if he sees suicide as his only way out of the bondage that holds him prisoner.

The list of "It's not our fault if…" could go on for pages. Whatever painful, difficult experiences we watch our kids go through, they aren't our fault. At least not completely. If we functioned as their ever-present safety net, shielding our adult children from the consequences of their choices, then perhaps some of the fault does rest on our shoulders.

So, if we aren't doing so already, we need to let our adult children deal with the consequences of their actions insofar as they are emotionally and mentally able to do so. Therein lies the challenge for us parents of troubled adult kids. How emotionally and mentally capable are they? What can they actually handle? Get that professional diagnosis and prognosis before you completely revamp your parenting.

In general, though, we parents must stop being safety nets. We must stop catching our falling children before they hit hard times and get banged up. And there is nothing easy about making this change.

The Prodigal Child

Jesus told the story of a father who let his troubled adult child experience the consequences of his foolish decisions. I'm going to offer an updated variation of it here.

One day his younger son demanded his inheritance and freedom from all his family obligations. The father was brokenhearted. He'd always given the child everything he needed. He'd raised him well and loved him with his whole heart. But it was never enough. Nothing the father did was ever sufficient for this son. So, despite knowing the dangers his son might face, the father let him go. He knew the boy could die. He knew he might never see his son again, but he also knew that he would never have a good relationship with his son if he demanded that he stay home where he could protect him.

So this troubled adult child took his dad's money and drove to Vegas. He bought drugs with his new wealth, stayed high as many days as he could, and partied like his life didn't matter and as if there were no tomorrow.

But tomorrow did come, and he found himself lying in his own vomit. He was stinky, sick, and broke. He reached out to his "friends," but no one was friendly anymore. He had nothing but a shopping cart and a few belongings. Cold and hungry and desperate, he slept on a park bench. Memories of home began to flood his mind, and he wondered if he could ever go back. He found a pay phone and a quarter, and he called home. When his mom answered, she heard these words: "Mom, I'm ready to get some help. I don't want to be this way anymore."

We know the wonderful rest of Jesus's story. Broken and repentant, the son returned home, wanting nothing more than to be a servant in his father's house. This young man knew he no longer deserved to be a child in this family. He was prepared to be a servant.

But the father had never given up hope for his boy. He had continued to pray and believe and watch for his son to return and be restored to the family. The father did not go looking for his son, though. He didn't send out a search party to bring him back. This father prayed. And this father waited.

You may have to wait too.

EFFECTIVE STRATEGY

Put your house rules in writing.

Appendix A is a template for a Residential Agreement. It isn't a one-size-fits-all document, but it may help you get started. You will need to make it your own. The responsibilities, expectations, and house rules will be specific to your troubled adult child and your family. Clearly state the consequences—and only include consequences that you are willing to enforce. You can also find a downloadable PDF of this form on my website at AllisonBottke.com. There is also a sample letter in Appendix B that may help you open the lines of communication with your child as you convey the changes you are going to implement in your house.

Chapter 17

When Is It Time to Let Go?

A day doesn't go by when I don't hear from a parent (or grandparent) who is struggling not only to survive, but to effectively help their addicted children or their emotionally or mentally ill children navigate the labyrinth of life.

There is an internal battle raging within the hearts of countless parents. The battle between the profound love we have for our adult children and our gut instincts about what action steps would be best for us and for them. We find ourselves torn between feeling obligated to help our troubled adult children and yearning to set them free, to cut the cord, so they can learn to live a healthy, independent, and self-sufficient life without our interference. Perhaps you frequently say to yourself, "My head tells me to let go of my troubled adult child, but my heart tells me to never let go." Maybe you also feel trapped in an ever-spinning cycle of guilt, shame, self-doubt, fear, anger, and confusion.

You are not unique in any of this warfare. How *do* we moms and dads call a truce between our heart and our head, between what we *feel* we should do and what we *know* we should do concerning our adult children?

The head/heart connection is definitely the battleground when we try to separate the love we have for our adult child from the wisdom and boundaries we know we must apply to our relationships with them. We can feel backed into a corner, compelled to intervene, and/

or confused about what we should do and when we should do it. We may vacillate between these two opposing thoughts:

1. If I help just one more time, this could be the turning point that will motivate my son to change and make better choices.

2. When will this end? I can't continue this cycle of digging my daughter out of yet another ditch. When will she develop the skill to climb out under her own power?

And so we become a prisoner on the gerbil wheel of insanity. We are going around and around and around—but not getting anywhere.

The Good News

You and I don't have to stop loving our children, but we do have to *change the way we love them.*

And there is even more good news. We already have the tools and experience we need to tackle this problem. After all, we've been changing the way we show our kids love from the time they were born.

When they were infants, we talked to them in baby talk, smooched all over them, diapered them, and tucked them in snugly. When they became toddlers, we put up baby gates and taught them to feed themselves. Sure, it was messy, but we loved them enough to let them miss their mouths at first but eventually learn to pilot their spoons accurately. When they walked away from us and into a kindergarten classroom of peers for the first time, we reluctantly let them go. The separation was difficult for both of us, and we both probably cried a little.

Years later we watched and waved as they drove down the street on their way to pick up a date, meet friends for a movie, or attend a school dance. Clearly, we know how to change the way we love our kids, and we know how to establish and enforce age-appropriate boundaries. We knew when it was time to stop the baby talk, to offer the spoon, to release them to their teacher, and to hand them the car keys. We truly know how to adjust the way we love our kids. We also know how and when to let go. At least we did.

And if we are honest with ourselves, we know that we really should have cut the umbilical cord, snipped the purse strings, and removed the emotional handcuffs long before now. It's going to be harder than it would have been if we had done it at the appropriate time. Most things that we put off until later are. It is hard, but not impossible. Besides, we are on a rescue mission. We would do anything—including letting them go—to save them. Wouldn't we?

But the Cycle Begins Subtly...

Taking her four-year-old son Jason with her, Patty left her abusive husband after years of physical, mental, and emotional abuse; she had finally had enough. Soon after, she met Alan, and they were married a few months later. Alan adopted Jason after years of struggling with Patty's ex-husband for child support. Jason's biological dad had very little contact with him, and at first it seemed that Alan and Jason were going to get along very well. Everyone said Alan was "just what Jason needed in a dad."

But Jason was not an easy kid to raise, and Alan had had no kids of his own. Jason was eventually diagnosed with ADHD, but even with his medication, Jason was very difficult for Patty and Alan to handle. When Jason was in his early teens, the trouble really started. Jason had developed a taste for pornography and alcohol. Although he was playing football for the city team, his grades were always hovering near F, and his relationship with Alan was becoming tense. A military man, Alan had a "shape up or ship out" attitude. Sadly, he and Jason had many verbal and physical altercations over the years.

The summer after Jason graduated from high school, he was arrested for being a Peeping Tom. Jason convinced Patty and Alan that it was "just a prank," a "one-time deal," and of course it would "never happen again." And it didn't. But within a year of that first arrest, he was arrested again. This time for a DUI and for driving with a suspended license. Jason hadn't paid some speeding tickets (that he hadn't told his folks about) and was driving recklessly when the officer pulled him over. He was arrested, and his parents bailed him out and paid his fines.

The next time Jason was arrested, it was for home invasion with a firearm. A felony conviction. Jason told his parents it was "mistaken identity," that "someone was wearing his clothes, and he was nowhere near the scene of the crime." With the help of his mother, who wrote a letter to the judge pleading for mercy for her son, Jason's sentence and his fines were greatly reduced. Still, he was sentenced to three years in prison. A powerful lesson, one would think.

Shortly after his release, Jason was stopped by the police for driving under the influence. Again, Jason was arrested, again his parents put up bail, and again his mother wrote a heartbreaking letter to the judge. Well, I'm sure you know how the rest of the story goes...

Yes, again the judge gave Jason a reduced sentence. However, this time in addition to paying fines and court costs, he would have to go to DUI school and do community service. All of which his parents paid for. His parents also made elaborate excuses for Jason's inability to attend the classes regularly or complete his community service hours. Can you guess what happened six short months later? That's right. He was arrested again.

And so it goes...on and on...to this very day. But there's more. In between all his arrests, rehabs, multiple jobs, and various relationships, Jason has verbally abused his mother and physically assaulted his step-father. After one particularly brutal physical altercation, the police were called, Jason was arrested, and—true to form—his parents dropped the charges the next day.

Can you identify the point in time when Patty and Alan should have known it was time to let go? Why do you think they didn't recognize it? What emotions kept them from seeing clearly? To better understand *when* it is time to let go, let's look first at *why* it has become hard for us to identify when we *should*.

Where to Start

The first step in separating our emotional heart from our rational head—in separating the unending parental love we have for our children no matter their age from our need for safe and healthy boundaries—is to realize the two can cohabitate. Heart and head can live in the same space but be two different things.

We can love our kids in ways that truly help—not handicap—them. At the same time, we can learn how to set healthy boundaries that will prevent us from "overloving" them, from enabling them.

Once we have this understanding, we can get to work. By applying the *S* step in SANITY we can *STOP trying to change our troubled adult children and start changing ourselves.*

Gulp.

Getting to the Root

A heavy cloud of guilt, shame, fear, and pride can keep us from doing what we know we should do when we know we should do it, so we find ourselves trapped on the gerbil wheel of enabling. We feel guilty because we didn't do every aspect of parenting right. We feel shame because of what others will think of us because of the choices our troubled kids make. We are afraid that all our best efforts will result in the unthinkable. And our pride keeps us from going to the only One who can truly change us…and them.

Perhaps if Patty and Alan had taken Jason out of football and hired a tutor to help him improve his grades, he would have learned that there are consequences for our choices. When they bailed him out of jail, maybe if they had both informed him that this would be the *only* time they would do so and insisted he pay his own fines, Jason would have understood the seriousness of his poor choices. But by this point in Jason's life, Patty and Alan may have already been too enveloped in the cloud and too heavily burdened with guilt, shame, fear, and pride to see the solutions clearly. Sadly, that burden only gets larger, heavier, and more difficult to put down the longer we carry it.

Opening Our Eyes

Also complicating the head versus heart struggle is the fact that it's hard for some of us parents in pain to recognize and admit that who and what our children *used* to be is not who and what they are *now*. A metamorphosis has occurred, and we've not wanted to see it. Many of our adult children are emotionally, intellectually, psychologically, socially, and spiritually stunted. Many are so rebellious our hearts repeatedly break, and still others are dangerously fragile, hanging on to life by a thread. Some have become unrecognizable to us. Some have gone from smoking pot to selling it. From destroying their own lives to taking others with them, like their siblings, their peers, and even strangers. Their destructive behavior affects innocent bystanders when, for instance, driving under the influence results in a car accident. Many of these adult children have cost their parents their marriages, their jobs, their financial health, their sanity…and, in some cases, even their faith in God.

Our adult children's very costly "rebellious streak" isn't just a phase that will go away. But that doesn't mean they are lost causes. Far from it.

The Question to Ask

The time has passed to ask, "What in heaven's name has happened?" The question must now be, "What changes do I need to make so that I am able to love God in a healthy way, love myself in a healthy way, and love my adult child in a healthy way?" And may our good God use the specific suggestions in this book—the SANITY encouragement to Stop, Assemble, Nip, Implement, Trust, and Yield—toward that end.

"I Will Restore…"

As long as our adult children are alive, we can choose to believe the truth that there is still hope for them, hope for their redemption, salvation, and return. Restoring ruined dreams and reclaiming wasted years is what God does best. It's the topic of the prophet Joel's entire message: "I will restore to you the years that the swarming locust has eaten" (Joel 2:25 ESV).

Restoration is such an encouraging word to parents in pain. But to get to restoration, we must start with the truth of where we are. In many cases, restoration cannot begin in the lives of our troubled adult children until we let go and allow them to experience the natural consequences of their actions. And trust that God is in control.

Hope in God, Hope for Our Children

Clearly, we do not parent as people who have no hope. We have a

God who watches after our children—if we'll just get out of His way and let Him do the restoring.

We must pray for the strength to see our children as they are— not as they were—and to take the steps, with God's help, to reframe our thinking and change our perspective and, therefore, our parenting strategy.

When I finally learned (the hard way) that all my "helping" was really "handicapping" my only child, it about broke my heart—and I realized things would never change—unless I did.

It wasn't easy. However, after years of running myself ragged on a vicious gerbil wheel of insanity, with God's help and wisdom and a willingness to shift the focus off my son and onto my own issues, I managed to find hope, healing, and sanity.

And I believe you can too.

Change begins when we apply the *Y* step in SANITY and YIELD ourselves to God and let the character of Christ flow from our hearts into theirs. Let God do the work. He has His hand on our troubled children, even if they don't see or feel it.

God will also help us assure our children that each and every one of us has had hurdles to overcome, that we all need to learn how to trust God and make our own way in the world despite our limitations. And may we assure our children—not just with our words but with how we live—that God is standing by them, ever ready to pour His help, healing, and hope into their troubled lives. Christian hope is the confident assurance that God will do what He says He will do. As believers, we can count on God's promises and find hope.

A Final Word

Dear parents, it's never too late to develop meaningful connections with our struggling adult children. No matter how dark and dangerous their world has become, we must never ever forget that God will always make a way when there seems to be no way.

Let us speak words of Christian hope and love into the hearts and minds of our troubled children. Together, we can travel through this valley of fear and pain and one day know true hope and healing.

Shalom, dear brothers and sisters in Christ,

Allison

Visit the SANITY Support section on my website to connect with me and other parents just like us. AllisonBottke.com

---

SANITY Support—
Residential Agreement

Between Parents and Adult Children Living at Home

Instructions: Below is a template to use in the development of your Residential Agreement. If you have additional or more specific requirements, incorporate them into your contract. You may create your contract using this information, or photocopy these pages and check the applicable boxes and fill in the blanks. You can also visit my website for a free downloadable PDF of this Residential Agreement at AllisonBottke.com.

Remember, this contract is for *house rules*, not *life rules*. As much as you may want your child to change the way he or she lives, you cannot control the lifestyle choices they make. Life rules include the choices we make about religion, education, eating right, exercising, what we choose to read, the type of friendships we forge, developing personal goals, and a host of positive and negative choices that comprise who we are as people. While you can encourage your adult child to establish personal life goals and perhaps develop their own "life plan," these areas of concern do not belong in your Residential Agreement.

When we are discussing and signing this agreement, we need to clarify that establishing house rules with a Residential Agreement contract isn't an attempt to control our children's lives. Try to communicate the big difference between house rules and life rules and acknowledge that we parents can't set rules for how our adult child chooses to live. However, we can—and we should—set rules for their behavior in *our* home and consequences when those rules are broken.

Again, clarify that you're not coming up with all these rules to punish or demean your child, but to reduce and eliminate stress. Explain that you desire to establish an atmosphere of hope and healing in the home that will promote family harmony as well as your child's success.

Dear Parents,

There are no cookie-cutter answers or remedies to the challenges we face concerning our troubled adult children.

Yes, I believe that God will make a way when there seems to be no way. I also believe that God doesn't want us to passively sit back and wait for something miraculous to happen. He wants us to claim His blessings and fruit—to make good (and godly) choices—and to walk in the power of His Word and wisdom.

It's time to stop being victims. To stop allowing our troubled adult children to control the narrative and instead decide what we, as parents, are ready, willing, and able to do.

And more important, to understand what role God is calling us to in the lives of our children.

My prayer is that you will be empowered to jump off the gerbil-wheel of insanity that has kept you repeating the same behaviors and instead adopt a new strategy for connecting with your adult child. A strategy that will release you from the bondage of enabling and set you on a new course to be the person—and the parent—God is calling you to be.

SANITY is possible, and I know you can find it!

Allison

SANITY Support - Residential Agreement
Between Parents and Adult Children Living at Home

As the parent(s), I/we seek to maintain a home atmosphere that is comfortable for everyone. This atmosphere needs to be guided by the mutual respect and concern of individual family members for one another.

The guidelines below are designed to maintain a sense of order and comfort for the parent(s), the adult child, and anyone else living in the home.

Any change or addition to this contract must be agreed to in writing and initialed by both the parent(s) and the adult child. If a change is not agreed to in writing and is not initialed by both the parent(s) and the adult child, it is not enforceable by the parent(s).

Residential agreement and responsibility contract between:

the PARENT(S) _____ and

the ADULT CHILD _____

Date signed:

Section #1: Purpose of This Agreement
The Adult Child is living with the Parent(s):

- ☐ So they can save money to buy property
- ☐ While dealing with personal or health issues
- ☐ While enrolled in school
- ☐ While looking for full-time employment that will allow independence
- ☐ While on probation, which expires on _____
  (insert date)
- ☐ While looking for full-time employment
- ☐ Other: _____

Section #2: Length of this Agreement

This agreement starts on: _____ (insert date)

This agreement is:

☐ On a month-to-month basis

☐ For a fixed length of time ending on _____
(insert date)

At the end of this fixed length of time:

☐ … the agreement may continue on a month-to-month basis or another fixed length of time, as identified in writing and signed by both parent(s) and adult child(ren)

☐ … the agreement ends, and the adult child must move out of the parental home

Section #3: Rent

The adult child will pay the rent of $_____ each month to the parent(s) on the first day of the month. The adult child must pay the rent on time or (insert consequence: eviction, loss of privileges, or _____ , etc.).

When the adult child gets a job, rent will be ___% of their income, to a maximum of $_____.

Instead of rent, the adult child must: _____

_____

(Insert tasks and be specific with time frame and expectations.) Remember, no one is paid to do basic household chores and maintenance. However, if you pay a vendor to conduct extra things like regular lawn care, dog walking, painting projects, or some other specific task that your adult child is capable of providing in a timely and acceptable manner, you may consider this service in lieu of rent. (Discuss possible opportunities with your adult child, and don't arbitrarily assign these work-for-hire jobs.)

Section #4: Household Expenses

In recognition that they are adding to the household expenses, the adult child agrees to contribute to the following expenses:

- ☐ Electricity (adult child to pay $_____ or _____ % of bill)
- ☐ Cable TV (adult child to pay $_____ or _____ % of bill)
- ☐ Heat (adult child to pay $_____ or _____ % of bill)
- ☐ Laundry facilities (adult child to pay $_____ or _____ % of bill)
- ☐ Health Insurance (adult child to pay $_____ or _____ % of bill)
- ☐ Parking for _____ vehicle(s) ($____)
- ☐ _____ (adult child to pay $_____ or _____ % of bill)
- ☐ _____ (adult child to pay $_____ or _____ % of bill)
- ☐ _____ (adult child to pay $_____ or _____ % of bill)

Food:
The adult child will:

- ☐ Pay $_____ per week toward the household food bill
- ☐ Be responsible for buying all of their own food

Personal Expenses:
The adult child will be responsible for the following personal expenses:

- ☐ Their own clothing costs
- ☐ Their own personal costs:

_____

_____

_____

Use of Family Vehicle:

☐ The adult child cannot use the family vehicle.

☐ The adult child can use the family vehicle under the following conditions:

    ☐ They may use the car only with advance notice and permission.

    ☐ They must return the car with a full tank of gas.

    ☐ They are responsible for any repair bills due to accidents or negligence.

    ☐ They must contribute _____% toward any routine maintenance.

    ☐ They must contribute $_____ or ___% toward increased insurance costs.

    ☐ They must contribute $_____ per month toward general maintenance and upkeep.

    ☐ They agree never to drink and drive.

Section #5: Responsibilities and Chores

The adult child shall:

☐ Keep their room or living space clean and tidy and in good repair

☐ Do their own laundry

☐ Be responsible for cooking family meals ___ days a week

☐ Provide the following pet care: _____

☐ Perform the following yard work/household chores:

_____

☐ Other chores: _____

Section #6: Household Rules

The adult child will respect the property of the parents and others living in the home, and behave in a manner that reflects a concern for others' safety and well-being.

It is agreed that the adult child will refrain from:

- ☐ Drunkenness in the home
- ☐ Swearing or use of profane language
- ☐ The use of tobacco in any form inside the home
- ☐ If permitted to smoke outside, cigarette butts must be disposed of in a proper receptacle
- ☐ The possession or use of marijuana and any drugs in the home
- ☐ Excessive noise, including music, between the hours of _____ and _____

Guests are:
- ☐ Not allowed
- ☐ Allowed under the following conditions: _____ _____ _____

Overnight guests are:
- ☐ Not allowed
- ☐ Allowed under the following conditions: _____ _____ _____

Section #7: Shared Resources

Family resources, such as the TV and computer, must be shared in a respectful and fair manner. The adult child is free to use the following household resources, under the following conditions:

Family Computer:

- ☐ For up to _____ hours a day
- ☐ Only for school and studying
- ☐ Only for searching for and applying for work
- ☐ With the following restrictions: _____
  _____
  _____

Family TV:

- ☐ For up to _____ hours a day
- ☐ The following programs (or type of programs) are not permitted: _____
  _____
  _____

Others:

  _____
  _____
  _____

Section #8: Privacy

In recognition that the adult child deserves a reasonable level of independence, the parent(s) agree to:

- ☐ Not enter the adult child's room/living space for any reason (other than exceptions listed below in Part 2)
- ☐ Not open any mail addressed to the adult child
- ☐ Others:

  _____
  _____
  _____

In recognition that the parent(s) deserve a reasonable level of privacy, the adult child agrees to:

- ☐ Not enter the parents' room/living space for any reason
- ☐ Not permit their guest(s) to enter the parents' room/living space for any reason
- ☐ Not open any mail addressed to the parent
- ☐ Others:

_____

_____

_____

PART 2: AIDING THE ADULT CHILD'S RECOVERY

In cases where the adult child is living in the parents' home to give them a safe place to deal with personal or health issues, including recovering from substance abuse or treating emotional and/or mental illness, specific challenges need to be addressed and agreed to.

While each situation is unique, this page is a starting place to make sure each party understands the rules and agrees to the special conditions this circumstance demands.

The adult child agrees to:

- ☐ Not use or possess any illegal drugs
- ☐ Not use or possess any alcohol
- ☐ Attend counseling sessions _____ times a week
- ☐ Attend support groups _____ times a week
- ☐ Obtain a professional diagnosis and prognosis from a reputable mental health provider and share written results with parent(s)

☐ Take prescribed medication at established times:

    ☐ Self-dispensed

    ☐ Dispensed by parent(s)

☐ Other: _____

_____

_____

If any of these agreements are broken, the consequence(s) will be: (Clearly identify each topic and the associated consequence. Be very specific.)

    _____

    _____

    _____

To enforce this agreement, the parent may:

☐ Enter the adult child's room/living space to confirm that no forbidden substances are in the home. This includes searching personal property.

☐ Access and review cell phone messages and texts

☐ Insist on an immediate blood test and/or urinary analysis

☐ Establish mandatory blood tests and/or urinary analysis:

    ☐ Weekly

    ☐ Monthly

☐ Other: _____

_____

_____

PART 3: WHEN THE ADULT CHILD IS ALSO A PARENT

If the adult child has children of their own in the parents' home, the following rules apply:

(Clearly identify all of the specific issues applicable to your situation.)

_____

_____

_____

_____

_____

_____

_____

End of Residential Agreement

Once again, this Residential Agreement is available as a downloadable PDF on my website at AllisonBottke.com. Look under the SANITY Support section for additional resources.

Personal Life Goals:

While the development of personal life goals is *not* part of the Residential Agreement, we can encourage our adult children to consider thinking about their future in a positive way.

Remember, no matter their struggles, our sons and daughters need to be treated like people, not problems. In addition to having food, clothing, and a place to live, our children also need purpose and hope. So consider ways to communicate with your child that might lead to a discussion about his or her goals and dreams—and listen.

We want our children to have bright futures, even if that dream seems distant or even impossible. We want to impact and influence their lives so that they can change their path, their attitude, and their trajectory.

To that end, let's encourage (not force) our adult children to identify their dreams, set goals, and begin to hope for those possibilities to become realities.

And the hope that our faith would impact our children is one reason why we must stand strong in our trust that God will keep His great promises regarding our trials and our children's future.

Appendix B

Sample Letters

Topics

1. Presenting a New Residential Agreement

2. Offer to Pay for Initial Mental Health Assessment or Provide Assistance in Applying for Financial Aid to Obtain a Diagnosis and Prognosis

3. Substance Abuse Concern and Desire to Help

The following letters can be downloaded from my website at AllisonBottke.com

1. Messy Child Not Contributing to Household

2. Time for Spoiled Child to Prepare to Move Out

3. Angry and Dangerous Adult Child Must Leave

4. No to Child Leaving Prison and Wanting to Live at Home

5. Yes to Child Leaving Prison and Wanting to Live at Home, But Must Sign Residential Agreement

6. Offering Full or Temporary Custody of Grandchildren If Child Moves Out to Get Help

7. Request That Unbelieving Child Not Disparage Parent's Faith

8. Ask Spouse Who Denies Adult Child's Problem to Meet with Professional

9. Ex-Spouse Doesn't Recognize How He/She Is Undermining Efforts to Help Child

10. Encouragement for a Grandchild Living with Addicted/ Mentally Ill Parents

11. Let Dangerous Adult Child Know You Can No Longer Be in Contact

Letter #1: Presenting a New Residential Agreement

Dear (son or daughter):

I want you to know how important you are to me. I value our relationship and want it to be the best it can be. For that to happen, certain changes must take place.

Please know that my choice to write this letter is not to avoid a personal conversation with you. But I know myself, and I know that in the past I haven't always conveyed my thoughts or feelings in a calm way, and for that I apologize. This letter allows me to express myself carefully. I can be more confident that I'm saying what I want to say.

I also want to apologize for trying to change you. You're an adult, and the life choices you make are yours. I have realized the only person I can change is myself, so I am working to develop effective strategies to do that in a more proactive way. As I begin to implement necessary changes in my life, some of those changes will undoubtedly impact you. One of those necessary changes is a Residential Agreement I have developed for both of us to follow and sign.

(Name), I have realized that, for the past (months/years), I have been doing you a disservice. By allowing you to live here without assuming any responsibilities or making any financial contributions to this household, I have been treating you like a child, treating you as if you were still eight years old. I have

not been encouraging you to become the best (man/woman) you can be, and for that I am truly sorry. I'm hoping we can sit down together, perhaps over a meal, and review the requirements and consequences outlined in this Residential Agreement that I'm putting into place because I love you and because I want the best for both of us.

Letter #2: Offer to Pay for Initial Mental Health Assessment or Provide Assistance in Applying for Financial Aid to Obtain a Diagnosis and Prognosis

Dear (son or daughter):

It breaks my heart to see you struggling with such (sadness, anger, and fear, etc.), and I want to help you find help. I know that somewhere inside you is a (man/woman) with great potential who's too tired, too depressed, and too frustrated to break free of the bondage. And I want to help you find freedom.

We've been hobbling along, doing our best to run this race together, but it's as if we're running in place. We've tried to do this on our own, but you need help that only a medical professional can give, starting with a diagnosis, prognosis, and maybe even medicine. I know you don't agree, but please hear me out.

I cannot and will not continue living in this drama and with this pain. You must get help. I will support you in ways I have identified in writing, including how much time and financial resources I am ready, willing, and able to extend in order to provide assistance and help you navigate this new terrain of care and support options.

However, if you choose not to get help, I cannot allow you to live with us anymore. I'm not being unkind or a bad parent. I want to see you healthy and whole and productive. I want what's best for you, what's best for all of us. You are an adult now, and I am determined to start treating you like one. I love you too much not to.

Letter #3: Substance Abuse Concern and Desire to Help

Dear (son or daughter):

I'm worried about you. I am watching you spiral out of control, addicted to drugs that may one day take your life or someone else's life in an accident.

I don't know what pain you're trying to numb or what caused you to get involved in this self-destruction, but I know one thing for sure. The son/daughter I used to know still exists inside you. I love that person very much, and I know that person has the potential to do great things. But before you can do that, you have to take the steps necessary to be free of this addiction that is robbing you of a full life.

I am very aware that I haven't always spoken my concerns to you with love. I've been angry, hurt, and confused by your decisions. But I know you need help, and I know you can't do this without support. So I want to sit down with you and talk about ways we can work together for positive change.

Parents, when you share this letter verbally with your troubled adult child, also be prepared to share specific ways you are ready, willing, and able to help—including financial assistance. Put everything in writing, including the consequences should they reject your offer.

There are more Sample Letters on my website at AllisonBottke.com.

Notes

Chapter 1—This Isn't How Life Is Supposed to Be

1. "Overdose Death Rates," National Institute on Drug Abuse, revised September 2017, www.dru gabuse.gov/related-topics/trends-statistics/overdose-death-rates

2. James Winnefeld, "A Scourge That Spares No Family," *The Week*, January 12, 2018, 41.

3. Jerry Mitchell, "With 175 Americans Dying a Day, What Are the Solutions to the Opioid Epidemic?" *USA Today,* Jan. 29, 2018 www.usatoday.com/story/news/nation-now/2018/01/29/175-americans-dying-day-what-solutions-opioid-epidemic/1074336001/

Chapter 2—Taking Rightful Control...of Your Home, Your Story, Your Life

1. Tony Evans, *30 Days to Overcoming Emotional Strongholds* (Eugene, OR: Harvest House, 2015), 9.

2. Reinhold Niebuhr, https://en.wikiquote.org/wiki/Reinhold_Niebuhr

Chapter 3—SANITY Strategies: Stop, Assemble, Nip, Implement, Trust, Yield

1. Henry Blackaby and Claude King, *Experiencing God* (Nashville, TN: B&H Publishing Group, 2004), 187.

2. Ibid., 163.

3. Allison Bottke, *Setting Boundaries with Your Adult Children* (Eugene, OR: Harvest House, 2008), 146.

Chapter 4—Experiencing Spiritual Growth and Establishing Healthy Boundaries

1. Henry Cloud and John Townsend, *How People Grow* (Grand Rapids, MI: Zondervan, 2001), 21-22.

2. Henry Cloud and John Townsend, *Boundaries* (Grand Rapids, MI: Zondervan, 1992), 27.

3. Bill Gaultiere, "Jesus Set Boundaries," Soul Shepherding (blog), July 20, 1998, http://www.soulshepherding.org/1998/07/jesus-set-boundaries/

Chapter 7—Befuddled Brains—Substance Abuse and Mental Illness

1. "How to Stop Enabling My Drug-Addicted Adult Child," The Treatment Center, February 17, 2017, https://ttccare.com/blog/how-to-stop-enabling-my-drug-addicted-adult-child/

2. "CDC Report: Mental Illness Surveillance Among Adults in the United States," Centers for Disease Control and Prevention, December 2, 2011, http://www.cdc.gov/mentalhealthsurveillance/fact_sheet.html

3. www.nami.org

4. www.afsp.org/about-suicide

5. June Hunt, *Counseling Through Your Bible: Providing Biblical Hope and Practical Help for 50 Everyday Problems* (Eugene, OR: Harvest House Publishers, 2008), 225.

Chapter 8—Diagnosis and Prognosis

1. NAMI, "Anosognosia," March 2015.

Chapter 9—Dangerous and Defiant

1. Sue Klebold, *A Mother's Reckoning: Living in the Aftermath of Tragedy* (New York: Crown Publishers, 2016), 32-33.

Chapter 10—Connecting Can Be Complicated

1. Lorie Konish with CNBC.com quoted in "Giving money to your adult children," *The Week*, January 26, 2018, https://www.pressreader.com/usa/the-week-us/20180126/282437054534069

2. Diane Harris with Forbes.com quoted in "Giving money to your adult children," *The Week*, January 26, 2018, https://www.pressreader.com/usa/the-week us/20180126/282437054534069

3. Suze Orman, "Managing Money" *The Costco Connection* 33, January 2018, 17.

4. "The mystery of America's missing male workers," *The Week*, November 5, 2016, http://theweek.com/articles/659245/mystery-americas-missing-male-workers

5. Ibid.

6. Ibid.

7. Ibid.

8. Carol Kent, *Waiting Together, Hope and Healing for Families of Prisoners* (Grand Rapids, MI: Discovery House, 2015), 46.

9. Brandon Gaille, "23 Statistics on Grandparents Raising Grandchildren," Brandon Gaille Marketing Expert&Blogmaster(blog),May22,2017,https://brandongaille.com/23-statistics-on-grandparents-raising-grandchildren/

10. Ibid.

11. Ibid.

12. "Kinship Caregivers/Grandparents Raising Grandchildren/Custodial Relatives," Connecticut 2-1-1, November 2017, http://uwc.211ct.org/kinship-caregiversgrandparents-raising-grandchildren custodial-relatives/

13. Charles Rubin, *Don't Let Your Kids Kill You: A Guide for Parents of Drug and Alcohol Addicted Children* (Petaluma, CA: New Century Publishers, 2007), 113-14.

14. Ibid.

15. "Stepfamily Statistics," The Stepfamily Foundation, accessed May 12, 2018, http://www.stepfamily.org/stepfamily-statistics.html

Chapter 11—Connecting Needs to Be Compassionate

1. Dr. Henry Cloud and Dr. John Townsend, *How People Grow* (Grand Rapids, MI: Zondervan, 2001), 200.

Chapter 12—The Power of Love and Forgiveness

1. Judy Hampton, *Ready? Set? Go!: How Parents of Prodigals Can Get On with Their Lives* (Hats Off Books, 2005), 94.

2. Stormie Omartian, *Seven Prayers That Will Change Your Life Forever* (Nashville, TN: Thomas Nelson, 2010), 45-46.

3. Ibid., 59.

4. Ibid., 58.

5. Hampton, 91.

6. Jill Rigby, *Raising Respectful Children in a Disrespectful World* (Brentwood, TN: Howard Books, 2013), 48.

7. Henry Cloud and John Townsend, *Boundaries* (Grand Rapids, MI: Zondervan, 1992), 251-52.

Chapter 13—Tough Decisions for Healthy Transformation

1. Gina Schaak, Lisa Sloane, Francine Arienti, Andrew Zovistoski, *Priced Out: The Housing Crisis for People with Disabilities* (Boston: Technical Assistance Collaborative, 2017), 9.

2. Kevin Martone, "Affordable Housing for People with Disabilities: A Worsening Crisis," Melville Charitable Trust, December 13, 2017, https://melvilletrust.org/affordable-housing-for-people-with-disabilities-a-worsening-crisis/

Chapter 14—Healthy Support and Compassionate Communication

1. Alison Matas, "Parents' recourse limited when adult child develops mental illness," IndeOnline.com, August 15, 2013, http://www.indeonline.com/article/20130815/news/308159872

Chapter 15—When Your Troubled Adult Child Lives with You

1. https://www.fema.gov/about-agency

2. Dr. Henry Cloud and Dr. John Townsend, *How People Grow* (Grand Rapids, MI: Zondervan, 2001), 218.

3. Joel Young, *When Your Adult Child Breaks Your Heart: Coping with Mental Illness, Substance Abuse, and the Problems That Tear Families Apart* (Guilford, CT: Lyons Press, 2013), 46.

4. Ibid., 46.

Setting Boundaries
with Your Adult Children

A complementary book to *How to Connect with Your Troubled Adult Children*, this important and compassionate book from the creator of the successful God Allows U-Turns series is the first book in the bestselling Setting Boundaries series, designed to help parents and grandparents of the many adult children who continue to make life painful for their loved ones.

A tough-love book to help readers cope with challenging adult children, *Setting Boundaries® with Your Adult Children* will empower families by offering hope and healing through S.A.N.I.T.Y.—a six–step program to help parents regain control in their homes and in their lives.

> **S** = STOP Enabling and STOP the Flow of Money
> **A** = Assemble a Support Group
> **N** = Nip Excuses in the Bud
> **I** = Implement an Action Plan
> **T** = Trust Your Instincts
> **Y** = Yield Everything to God

Foreword by Carol Kent (*When I Lay My Isaac Down* and *Waiting Together*)

More from Allison Bottke

Setting Boundaries® for Women
Setting Boundaries® with Difficult People
Setting Boundaries® with Food
Setting Boundaries® with Your Adult Children
A Young Woman's Guide to Setting Boundaries

To learn more about Harvest House books and
to read sample chapters, visit our website:
www.harvesthousepublishers.com

HARVEST HOUSE PUBLISHERS
EUGENE, OREGON
